Moving Pictures

Moving Pictures

An Annotated Guide
to Selected Film Literature
With Suggestions for the
Study of Film

Eileen Sheahan

UPSALA COLLEGE LIBRARY
WIRTHS CAMPUS

South Brunswick and New York: A. S. Barnes and Company
London: Thomas Yoseloff Ltd

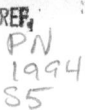

© 1979 by A. S. Barnes and Co., Inc.

A. S. Barnes and Co., Inc.
Cranbury, New Jersey 08512

Thomas Yoseloff Ltd
Magdalen House
136-148 Tooley Street
London SE1 2TT, England

Library of Congress Cataloging in Publication Data

Sheahan, Eileen.
  Moving pictures.

   1. Moving-pictures—Bibliography. I. Title.
Z5784.M9S5   1978   [PN1994]   016.79143   78-55576
ISBN 0-498-02296-X
ISBN 0-498-02297-8 pbk.

PRINTED IN THE UNITED STATES OF AMERICA

Contents

	Introduction	7
A.	Guides and Handbooks	13
B.	Dictionaries and Encyclopedias	17
C.	Annuals and Directories	23
	CA. Annuals	23
	CB. Directories	29
D.	Bibliographies and Catalogs	34
	DA. Books on Moving Pictures: Comprehensive Bibliographies	34
	DB. Books on Moving Pictures: Continuing Bibliographies	39
	DC. Books on Moving Pictures: Catalogs	40
	DD. Book Reviews	43
	DE. National Bibliographies	44
	England • France • Germany • Italy • United States	
E.	Film Lists and Sources	47
	EA. International Filmographies	47
	EB. National Filmographies	51
	Africa • Canada • China • Eastern Europe • England • France • Germany • Italy • Soviet Union • Sweden • United States	
	EC. Lists of Films of Individuals (Credits)	59
	ED. Film Catalogs	64
	EE. Film Scripts	68
	EF. Literary Sources and Film Adaptations	71
	EG. Plot Summaries	75
F.	Film Histories	77
	FA. International Film Histories	77
	FB. National Film Histories	81
	Africa • China • Eastern Europe • England • France • Germany • India • Italy • Japan • Scandinavia • Soviet Union • United States	

	FC.	Genre Studies and Partial Histories	90
		Blacks in Moving Pictures • Documentary Films • Fantasy in Moving Pictures • Music and Musicals • Mystery, Crime, Spy Films • Serials • Special Effects • Underground Film • Westerns • Women in Moving Pictures	
	FD.	Basic Studies of Theory and Technique	99
		Theory and Aesthetics • Technique	
G.	Biography	104
H.	Film Reviews and Criticism	111
I.	Periodicals	116
	IA.	Selection of Important Film Periodicals	116
	IB.	Periodical Lists	119
	IC.	Periodical Indexes	121
		Film Periodical Indexes • General Indexes	
	ID.	Periodical Locations	128
J.	Dissertations	129
	Index		
		Subject Index	
		Author/Title Index	

Introduction

Entertainment was once the main attraction for moviegoers, but today's devotees look for the director's style. We speak now of "film" and "cinema" as readily as the "movies," largely because contemporary criticism has prompted us to regard moving pictures as a sophisticated art form. Interest in film has always encouraged publishing; books about film are now proliferating, and film books seem to beget more film books.

This book is a starting place for research in the literature of film, compiled to guide the film researcher through a large and complex subject. It was inspired by some confused college students who suddenly had to write papers for a film course when all they had wanted was to see some good movies.

Until now there has been no selective guide to key reference sources in film study that provides both explanation and quick access to all subjects, authors, and titles. This guide should be of value to anyone near a good-sized library, since many of the publications included are generally available.

Those who are not near good film collections can improve the situation through the various systems of library cooperation. Ask a librarian about the possibilities in your area.

Organization

Most of the titles in this guide are reference books—encyclopedias, bibliographies, indexes, histories—grouped broadly by type. Periodicals are also included because of their importance to film research. The table of contents serves as an outline. Consult the index for detailed subject approaches as well as for particular authors and titles. Many works offer a variety of information yet must be fitted into a single category; they are cross-referenced in other sections.

Scope

Publications from early film writings to books published through mid-1977 are included in this guide. Some general reference works that most libraries would have are also described.

Emphasis is on English-language publications, but foreign-language works that have no counterpart are also included. Even if you know no foreign languages, do not avoid the magnificent *Enciclopedia dello spettacolo* (nos. B6–B9) and *Filmlexicon degli autori* (no. G4), or the French film histories (Section FA). They can provide much assistance through their bibliographies and filmographies and are surprisingly easy to follow—particularly with a dictionary.

Screenplays, monographs on films or individuals, collected criticism, interview and how-to-do-it books are excluded. Since such works concern a single name, or a single topic, library catalogs provide direct access to the desired information. Collections of essays are also omitted. Though important for ideas and insights, they are not really reference sources.

As a result of these choices, some exceptional authors are absent from this guide.

Entries

Entries are arranged alphabetically by author, or by title, and are numbered sequentially within each section. Cross-references and the index refer to this item number.

Each entry is described. The annotation aims to explain the purpose of the work, to point out its reference features (bibliography, index, statistics, etc.), and to suggest its value for film research. Although critical judgments have been avoided, editorial comment is sometimes offered.

Acknowledgment

Originally this guide was written for students of film at Yale University and emphasized the University Library holdings. That edition has since traveled widely, and the many changes that were suggested along the way have been incorporated in this version.

Special mentor was Jay Leyda, former professor of film at Yale University, now at New York University. Important advice was also given by John Podeschi, book consultant, Stanley Kauffmann, film critic, and Howard Keith, film lover.

Gratitude is also due those people at the Yale University Library, Museum of Modern Art Library, Theater Collection of the New York Public Library, Educational Film Library Association, Drama Book Shop, Gotham Book Mart, University of Oregon Library, University of Tennessee Library, Canadian Film Institute, Theater Library of the University of California at Los Angeles, Library of the Academy of Motion Picture Arts and Sciences, Larry Edmunds Bookshop, and Library of the University of California at Berkeley, who helped so much.

Particular thanks to Barbara Humphrys and Patrick Sheehan of the Motion Picture Section, Library of Congress.

Invitation

A book such as this—in fact any book that offers information—should be considered a draft that can be improved by those who use it. The author and publisher welcome all suggestions and advice.

Anyone who uses books develops strong prejudices about certain ones. Personal taste often influenced the process of selection here; hence some well-known works were omitted because the same information could be found elsewhere. Cool objectivity might be desired, but the subject of film encourages warm opinions not only in filmgoers, but also in the compiler of a guide such as this.

A. Guides and Handbooks

A research project in film studies can well begin with guides and handbooks. Manchel's *Film Study* (no. A6), which describes important books and articles as well as recommended films, is an excellent introduction to the subject. Bowles's *Approach to Film Study* (no. A1) and Limbacher's *Reference Guide to Audiovisual Information* (no. A5) list basic research books by subject area.

Handbooks such as Gottesman and Geduld's *Guidebook to Film* (no. A3) and Halliwell's *Filmgoer's Companion* (no. A4) collect general information that is also useful for orientation.

Bibliographies of books on moving pictures (Section D) can supplement these guides.

A1. Bowles, Stephen E. *An Approach to Film Study: A Selected Booklist.* Brooklyn, N.Y.: Revisionist Press, 1974.

Checklist of important film books, arranged by categories. Particularly useful for research in national cinemas, genre studies, theories of film art, individual critics, individual studies (arranged by subject's name). None of the titles are described. Section 8, individual films, groups film scripts, production accounts, and critical studies together by film title. English-language film periodicals arranged by emphasis. Includes foreign-language publications when nothing available in English. Addenda of late entries. Not indexed.

A2. Bukalski, Peter J., comp. *Film Research: A Critical Bibliography with Annotations and Essay.* Boston: G. K. Hall, 1972.

Briefly describes 50 "Essential Works" and lists 3,000 other film books in these categories: film history, theory, criticism; production and technology; genre; sociology and economics; national cinema; scripts; particular films; personalities, biographies, and filmographies; education; film-related works; bibliographies, guides, and indexes; selected works in foreign languages. Also names periodicals and sources for film rental and purchase. Not indexed.

A3. Gottesman, Ronald, and Geduld, Harry M. *Guidebook to Film: An Eleven-in-One Reference.* New York: Holt, Rinehart and Winston, 1972.

Convenient collection of information about moving pictures, although much is dated now. Most valuable for its bibliographies of books and dissertations. Paperback edition. In eleven parts:
1. Annotated list of books and periodicals, which briefly describes standard works in reference, history, theory, technique, etc.;
2. List of 489 theses and dissertations about film, written at 32 American universities between 1916 and 1969;
3. Directory of museums and archives dealing with film, grouped by continent;
4. Film schools in U.S. and other countries;
5. Equipment and supply sources in U.S.;
6. Distributors for film rentals and purchases in U.S.;
7. Bookstores, publishers, and sources for stills throughout world;
8. Film organizations and services, including major film studios of world;
9. Film festivals and contests in U.S. and other countries;
10. Chronologies of important film awards of U.S.;
11. Terminology, plus important abbreviations.

A4. Halliwell, Leslie. *The Filmgoer's Companion.* 4th ed.; entirely revised...much enlarged. New York: Hill and Wang, 1974.

Geared for general moviegoer rather than specialist. Arranges in one alphabet: names (performers, directors, producers, musicians, writers, photographers), processes, themes, subjects, terms, characters, film titles. An entry such as "Shakespeare," for instance, gives a history of films based on his work. International in coverage, with emphasis on American and English film. Separate indexes: films; fictional screen characters and series; themes explored; title changes—American to British and vice versa; performers in illustrations. Addenda. List of recommended books, pp. 849–51. Richly illustrated. Available in paperback (Avon Books, 1975). A 5th edition, *Halliwell's Filmgoer's Companion* (St. Albans, England: Paladin, 1976), adds death dates through 1974. No new information is added, however. An American 5th edition is due in 1977.

A5. Limbacher, James L. *A Reference Guide to Audiovisual Information.* New York: R. R. Bowker, 1972.

Intended for librarians who assist film researchers, this guide is of general interest. The section "Reference Works Indexed by Subject," pp. 65–82, provides answers to questions; e.g., "Actors—credits and filmographies" lists 56 sources for this information; "Reviews and ratings—theatrical films" lists 62 books and periodicals that review popular film. Other sections: books and periodicals essential for film study, briefly described; dictionary of audiovisual terms; publishers' addresses; selected bibliography of additional books. Lacks an overall index.

An earlier version (*A Reference Guide to Film Information;* Dearborn, Mich.: Henry Ford Centennial Library, 1971) is important for its appendices: I. "Remakes, Series and Sequels on Film and Television" (3d ed.: 1970. See no. EF8 for description); II. "Handbook for Film Societies" (2d ed.: 1969); III. "Selected List of Recorded Musical Scores from Radio, Television and Motion Pictures" (4th ed.: 1967).

A6. Manchel, Frank. *Film Study: A Resource Guide.* Rutherford, N.J.: Fairleigh Dickinson University Press, 1973.

A teaching guide that surveys approaches to the study of film as an art form. Valuable here for comments on recommended films, and books and articles on film. Provides glossary; lists reliable film critics, periodicals, distributors of 16mm and 8 mm film. Locate information through the indexes: article titles; authors— articles; authors—books; book titles; film personalities; film titles; subject.

A7. Monaco, James. *How to Read a Film: The Art, Technology, Language, History and Theory of Film and Media.* New York: Oxford University Press, 1977.

Included here for these reference features: bibliography, pp. 439–66, arranged in two parts: Part One: readings that correspond to the text's chapters; film history, including general historical studies, specific major periods, genres, national cinemas, films and filmmakers, filmscripts; film theory and criticism; Part Two: Film Information, a guide to research materials, encyclopedias, indexes, etc. Also provided: glossary for film and media criticism, which revises and expands Monaco's *Standard Glossary for Film Criticism* (see no. B15); a chronology of film and media; directory of important film journals in English. Available in paperback.

A8. Rehrauer, George. *The Film User's Handbook: A Basic Manual for Managing Library Film Services.* New York: R. R. Bowker, 1975.

Useful for anyone designing a film program. Discusses building the film collection, equipment selection, evaluation and use, organizing film service. Appendices: basic annotated bibliography; selected film periodicals; associations and organizations; film distributors; equipment manufacturers.

Samples, G. *How to Locate Reviews of Plays and Films.* Sections on film and reference guides. See no. H9.

A9. Steele, Robert Scott. *The Cataloging and Classification of Cinema Literature.* Metuchen, N.J.: Scarecrow Press, 1967.

Outlines classification schemes used by the Academy of Motion Picture Arts and Sciences, Canadian Film Institute Library, Museum of Modern Art Library, Library of Congress, and some other institutions. For one thing, these schemes can assist in locating obscure material. Bibliography; index.

A10. Toeplitz, Jerzy. "Film Scholarship: Present and Prospective." *Film Quarterly* 16, no. 3 (Spring 1963): 27–37.

Although old now, this article is still informative. Describes important reference books and sources; discusses research centers throughout the Western world, including film institutes, universities, and archives; outlines means for cooperation between scholars, naming the various international film federations. Excellent bibliography of works cited in the text.

A11. Weiner, Janet. *How to Organize and Run a Film Society.* New York: Macmillan Co., 1973.

Concise handbook for organizing and maintaining a film society. Lists distributors with their specialties. Film-source directory is arranged by films proven popular with societies. Important film bookshops in U.S., England, and Canada are described. Indexed. Paperback edition. A similar but older publication provides a critical, annotated bibliography: *Film Viewer's Handbook* by Emile G. McAnany and Robert Williams (Glen Rock, N.J.: Paulist Press, 1965). Paperback edition.

A12. Wrigley, Maurice Jackson, and Leyland, Eric. *The Cinema: Historical, Technical, and Bibliographical. A Survey for Librarians and Students.* London: Grafton & Co., 1939.

Useful for students of early film. Arranged by detailed subject areas; includes periodical articles. Appendices list periodicals and supply historical data.

B. Dictionaries and Encyclopedias

Consult dictionaries and encyclopedias for specific information. The main purpose of a *dictionary* is to define the meaning of words. Dictionaries of special terms such as the *Dictionary of Literary, Dramatic, and Cinematic Terms* (no. B1) and Monaco's *Standard Glossary for Film Criticism* (no. B15) supplement general dictionaries with more specific definitions. The polyglot dictionaries—Elsevier's *Dictionary of Cinema, Sound and Music* (no. B5) and Van Nooten's *Film Vocabulary* (no. B22)—can assist with reading articles in foreign languages.

Some dictionaries may also supply some encyclopedic information. Graham's *Dictionary of the Cinema* (no. B11) and Bessy and Chardans' *Dictionnaire du cinéma* (no. B2) are examples of this.

Encyclopedias generally have a broader scope, providing definitions, historical events, biographies, and illustrations. In addition, many offer a basic bibliography at the end of each entry. The very best set for film research is the multivolume *Enciclopedia dello spettacolo* (nos. B6-B9), and many facts can be gleaned with an Italian dictionary. But the one-volume *International Encyclopedia of Film* (no. B13) and *Oxford Companion to Film* (No. B16) are probably more accessible.

Two general works that are excellent starting places for any research are the *Encyclopedia Americana* and the *Encyclopedia Britannica*. Both have detailed indexes that indicate all pertinent material. Some European encyclopedias have outstanding illustrations and excellent bibliographies; the Italian *Enciclopedia italiana;* the French *Grand Larousse;* the German *Brockhaus' Konversations-Lexikon.*

Many biographical works (Section G) are encyclopedic in nature.

B1. Barnet, Sylvan: Berman, Morton; and Burto, William. *A Dictionary of Literary, Dramatic, and Cinematic Terms.* 2d ed. Boston: Little, Brown, 1971.

18 / Moving Pictures

Emphasizes literary terms, but includes concise definitions of cinematic terms. Many cross-references and suggested readings. Paperback edition.

B2. Bessy, Maurice, and Chardans, Jean-Louis. *Dictionnaire du cinéma et de la télévision.* 4 vols. Paris: J.-J. Pauvert, 1965–71.
Especially useful for its coverage of the history and technology of film industry. Gives biographical information about film and television personalities, including their credits. Illustrated. Defines English as well as French terms. A fifth volume, to include a "filmographie," is planned.

B3. Boussinot, Roger. *L'encyclopédie du cinéma.* 2 vols. Paris: Bordas, 1967–70.
First volume emphasizes films and personalities and includes terms, technical topics, film companies, brief surveys of national cinemas. Filmographies provided for performers and directors. Index to illustrations. Second volume (*L'encyclopédie du cinéma par l'image*) is a picture book of important films and film people. Arranged in one alphabet by name or title with descriptive caption for each selection. Film titles given in language of origin. Index to illustrations cites performers, directors, films illustrated in both volumes.

B4. Clarke, Charles G., and Strenge, Walter, eds. *American Cinematographer Manual.* 4th ed. Hollywood: American Society of Cinematographers, 1973.
An indispensable guide to technology of cinematography. Supplies information about equipment and technique, naming brands and models; provides tables; gives ASC recommendations. Also includes threading diagrams, glossary, and list of technical terms in five languages (English, Spanish, French, Italian, German). Table of contents lists everything alphabetically.
New developments summarized in *American Cinematographer: The International Journal of Motion Picture Photography and Production Techniques* (Los Angeles: 1919–; monthly).

B5. *Elsevier's Dictionary of Cinema, Sound and Music, in Six Languages: English/American, French, Spanish, Italian, Dutch and German.* Compiled and arranged by W. E. Clason. Amsterdam/New York: Elsevier Publishing Co., 1956.
Polyglot dictionary arranged by English-language word or term, with equivalents in French, Spanish, Italian, Dutch, and

German. Gives cross-references between British and American usage. Very thorough. Separate index for each language. Brief bibliography.

B6. *Enciclopedia dello spettacolo.* 9 vols. Rome: Casa Editrice le Maschere, 1954–62.

Treats the world of entertainment, including moving pictures, theater, opera, ballet, vaudeville, etc. Articles discuss performers, directors, writers, as well as genres, themes, and historical and technical subjects. The article "Colori," for instance, explains development and art of technicolor in film. The lengthy essay on "Cinema" concludes with a full bibliography, divided into reference sources, general history, and partial histories. Articles on individuals cite their films and provide brief bibliographies. Beautifully and profusely illustrated.

B7. ———. *Appendice di aggiornamento. Cinema.* Venice: Istituto per Collaborazione Culturale, 1963.

Updates *Enciclopedia* by adding film personalities not included in original set. Two sections: European and American directors and performers; and Italian scenarists, cameramen, designers, and musicians. Illustrated with movie stills.

B8. ———. *Aggiornamento 1955–1965.* Rome: Unione Editoriale, 1966.

Updates the main set by discussing developments and personalities, 1955–65.

B9. ———. *Indice-repertorio.* Rome: Unione Editoriale, 1968.

Index to titles (145,000 in all) of all works (films, plays, opera, ballets, etc.) mentioned in main set and two supplements, giving author, genre, and year of composition. All titles listed in original language, in one alphabet. Russian titles are transliterated (Italian transliteration used; e.g. "Uncle Vanya" is "Djadja Vanja"); Greek titles listed separately. The *Indice* forms a universal repertory of the performing arts, indexing titles and giving performance history.

B10. *Enciclopedia ilustrada del cine.* 4 vols. Barcelona: Editorial Labor, 1970.

Volumes 1 through 3 cover, in one alphabet: names of individuals, films, characters, national cinema, etc. Many entries include filmography. International in coverage, with emphasis on Spanish-language film. Also provides chronology of international film festivals (end of vol. 1) and technical vocabulary (end of vol. 3). Vol. 4 covers technical topics; concluded by indexes to films and to subjects and countries covered in first three volumes. Well illustrated.

B11. Graham, Peter. *A Dictionary of the Cinema.* International Film Guide Series. Rev. ed. South Brunswick and New York: A. S. Barnes and Co., Inc., 1968.

First section lists people involved in moving pictures—performers, directors, producers, etc. Second section defines technical terms. Index to all films cited.

B12. Levitan, Eli L. *An Alphabetical Guide to Motion Picture, Television and Videotape Production.* New York: McGraw-Hill Co., 1970.

Describes materials, equipment, processes, and techniques used in production. Illustrated with photographs, drawings, diagrams, charts. "Subject guide to entries" serves as index. Written primarily for the technician and researcher, but useful for casual reference because of its fairly nontechnical language.

B13. Manvell, Roger, and Jacobs, Lewis, eds. *The International Encyclopedia of Film.* New York: Crown Publishers, 1972.

First English-language encyclopedia of international film; concerned mainly with film as art. Lists biographies, national film histories, general topics, technical terms—in one alphabet. Also includes chronological outlines of film history and an excellent bibliography that includes reference books, filmmaking, film and society, theory and aesthetics, criticism, genre, general and national histories, individual studies. Abundantly illustrated. Indexes: title changes, of American films in England and vice versa; names; films (lists some 6,500 titles).

B14. Michael, Paul, *The American Movies Reference Book: The Sound Era.* Englewood Cliffs, N.J.: Prentice-Hall, 1969.

Guide to persons and films that have enjoyed the greatest success in Hollywood. In separate chapters: brief biographies and complete listing of English-language feature-sound films of 600 performers; credits and some interesting facts on 1,000 films; filmographies of 50 directors and 50 producers; chronologies of film awards, including Academy Awards, New York Film Critics, National Board of Review, Patsy Awards, *Film Daily's* Ten Best, *Photoplay* Gold Medal, and top-grossing films of each year.

Illustrated. Bibliography. Indexes to performers, directors, and producers include illustrations.

B15. Monaco, James. *A Standard Glossary for Film Criticism.* 2d ed. New York: New York Zoetrope, 1975.
Concerned only with terms used in English-language film criticism, excluding specialized and technical terms. Succinct definitions; booklet format. Has been revised and expanded in his *How to Read a Film* (see no. A7).

B16. *Oxford Companion to Film.* London/New York: Oxford University Press, 1976.
Edited by Liz-Anne Bawden, with contributions by fifty film experts. Dictionary of artists, craftsmen, critics, genres, movements, technical processes, histories of major film production companies. Around 700 individual films are discussed. Worldwide coverage. Articles on directors mention significant works; no complete filmographies. Beautifully illustrated with actual frame shots (rather than publicity stills). No bibliographies.

B17. Pasinetti, Francesco, comp. *Filmlexicon, piccola enciclopedia cinematografica.* Milan: Filmeuropa, 1948.
Dictionary in three parts: definitions of general and technical terms; brief biographies of people involved in film; detailed bibliography. Old, but still useful. Served as model for subsequent encyclopedias of film. Illustrated.

B18. Pessis-Pasternak, Guitta. *Dictionnaire du l'audio-visuel. Français-anglais et anglais-français.* Paris: Flammarion, 1976.
Gives equivalents in English and in French for vocabulary of film, photography, radio, television, video.

B19. Reinert, Charles, Hrsg. *Kleines Filmlexikon: Kunst, Technik, Geschichte, Biographie, Schrifttum.* Einsiedeln-Zurich: Beinziger & Co., 1946.
A predecessor of Pasinetti's *Filmlexicon,* above. Dictionary includes biographies, terms, and techniques; followed by bibliography that includes dissertations. Lists Swiss films made between 1933 and 1945.

B20. Sakharov, Aleksandr A. *English-Russian Dictionary of Photography and Cinematography.* Moscow: Foreign-Language Scientific and Technical Dictionaries, 1960.
Lists over 10,000 specialized terms used in English, with Russian equivalents. Index to Russian words and terms.

B21. Spottiswoode, Raymond, gen. ed. *Focal Encyclopedia of Film and Television Techniques.* New York: Hastings House, 1969.

Articles by specialists on techniques, terms, equipment for film and television. Topics arranged alphabetically with cross-references to broader or closely related subjects. Readings cited with many entries. Illustrated with line drawings and diagrams. Index.

B22. Van Nooten, S. I., comp. *Vocabulaire du cinéma / Film Vocabulary.* 6th ed. The Hague: Netherlands Information Service (not dated, probably 1973).

Published for the Council of Europe. Word list of approximately 900 cinematic terms, applicable to cultural and educational film and audiovisual education. Gives equivalent terms in French, English, Dutch, Italian, German, Spanish, Danish. For each language, terms are arranged by numerical and alphabetical lists (the French list establishes numbered order). One then cross-references between languages. Also includes conversion table for speed numbers and other technical equivalency tables.

B23. Winchester, Clarence, ed. *The World Film Encyclopedia: A Universal Screen Guide.* London: Amalgamated Press, 1933. (Reprinted: Gordon Press, 1976)

Probably the most comprehensive reference source for moving pictures in its day. Provides over 1,000 biographies, grouped by performers, directors, etc. Some sections: casts of 500 films made between 1922 and 1932; brief histories of film studios; directory of producing companies; dictionary of film terms; list of abbreviations. Illustrated; index.

C. Annuals and Directories

Although there is almost no difference between an annual and a directory, they are separated here because of the quantity. Both provide a quick answer to a question. Other than that, they can vary considerably from title to title.

CA. Annuals

Annuals update information about moving pictures on a continuing basis—generally every year. Some record just about everything that should be kept up-to-date: statistics, awards, new films and books. Examples are the *Film Daily Year Book* (no. CA10) and *International Motion Picture Almanac* (no. CA14).

They may record current developments, as do the *Film Review* (no. CA11), *International Film Guide* (no. CA13), and *Screen World* (no. CA20); or they may provide directories of persons or institutions, such as the *Audiovisual Market Place* (no. CA4), *Guide to College Courses in Film and Television* (no. CA12), and *Motion Picture Market Place* (no. CA16).

Many libraries will not have film annuals, but they will have the popular *Information Please Almanac* or *World Almanac*, which have a surprising amount of information—such as annual award winners, top-grossing films, and other statistics.

CA1. *Annuaire de cinéma et télévision.* Paris: Éditions Bellefaye, 1948–.

First issued in 1948; annual since 1950. Directory for all aspects of French film industry. Gives credits and brief synopsis of feature-length films presented in France during previous year. Also lists short films made in France. "Bibliographie Generale" is comprehensive list of works in the French language dedicated to film and television. Cites collective works; special issues of journals and reviews; annuals, manuals, guides, etc.; reports of congresses and official documents. Directory also includes photographic gallery of performers; winners of international festivals.

CA2. *Annuaire du spèctacle: cinéma, théatre, télévision et musique variétés.* Paris: Editions Raoult, 1942/1943–73.

Directory of French show business including film, radio, television. About one-third of volume is a photographic gallery of performers, mostly in French film and theater, with index of names. First section, Cinema, gives: directory of production companies, publicity agents, producers, writers, directors, all categories of technicians, distributors in Paris and in the provinces, exporters, press, professional organizations. Film festivals and prizes of the previous year are named. Lists films released in France during previous year, giving title in French and in original language, length, distributor, cast, brief plot summary. A similar section summarizes some of same information for the Common Market nations and for French-speaking Switzerland. Begins new format with volume for 1974.

CA3. *Annuario del cinema italiano.* Rome: Cinedizione, 1950/1951–.

Yearbook of Italian film production. Includes these sections: Italian film organizations and associations; directory of Italian film people, including film credits; "Film" (section III, in three parts) forms filmography of Italian films from 1930 through year of *Annuario*'s coverage (1973 for 1973/1974 volume): (1) all films listed alphabetically by title; (2) films arranged by year of production; (3) films from 1960 through year of coverage for which full information is given: studio, literary source, credits, major cast. This part can continue filmography in Lizzani's *Storia del cinema italiano* (see no. EB8).

CA4. *Audiovisual Market Place: A Multimedia Guide.* New York: R. R. Bowker, 1969–. Annual.

Directory emphasizes educational film, but includes entertainment film. Lists organizations, films, personnel, and provides buyer's guide. Excellent bibliography of reference books and directories, arranged by title, with classified index. Other useful features: directory of periodicals and review services; associations; music, sound-effects and stock-shot libraries; funding sources; American awards and festivals; glossary; etc. Index.

CA5. *British Film and Television Year Book.* London: British and American Press, 1946–. Annual.
Recently retitled *International Film and Television Yearbook;* formerly *British Film Yearbook.* Founded and edited by Peter Noble. Bulk of volume is "Who's Who in British Film and Television." Many American performers included. Provides directory of production companies, distributors, studios, laboratories, trade organizations, and so on. Also lists films released in previous year.

CA6. *Calendar of International Motion Picture and Television Events.* U.S. Information Agency, International Communications Media Staff. Washington, D.C.: USIA, May 1977.
Lists festivals, shows, etc. by continent, then by country. Revised annually. Further information about most events can be obtained from Council on International Nontheatrical Events (CINE/1201 Sixteenth St., N.W., Washington, D.C. 20036). The same office prints an annual *Calendar of Motion Picture and Television Events in the United States.*

CA7. Directors Guild of America. *Directory of Members.* Hollywood: 1967/1968–.
Gives address, and often the agent, of film and television directors, along with brief summary of their work or qualifications. Geographical and type index; index of agents, attorneys, business managers.

CA8. *Film Canadiana. The Canadian Film Institute Yearbook of Canadian Cinema.* Ottawa: Canadian Film Institute, 1972/1973–. Annual.
Currently compiled by Piers Handling, Louis Valenzuela, and Maynard Collins. Provides a comprehensive annual record of film in Canada. Filmography (which includes features, shorts, documentaries, television films) gives full credits plus summary of that year's films. 1975–76 edition has "Feature Film Index 1970–75." Production index to directors, performers, etc., follows filmography. Also includes: bibliography (periodicals and books); organizations; festivals and awards; statistics. Editorial index concludes volume.

CA9. *Film Daily Directors Annual and Production Guide.* New York: 1920–38. Annual.
"Designed as a mid-year supplemental reference work to the annual *Film Daily Year Book of Motion Pictures*" (see below).

Provides production program of each studio for that year. Brief biographies of directors and producers; lists work for that year of directors, screenwriters, film editors, cameramen, performers, song writers, etc.; names personnel of studios, associations, etc. Editorial index at front of volume.

This annual had a complicated history: Vols. 1 through 9 (1920–28) were published as the Sunday issue of *Film Daily*; years 1940–43 and 1946–48, issued as part of *Film Daily*; years not published: 1933, 1938–39, 1944–45. Also called: *Film Daily Production Guide and Directors Annual* (from 1934 through 1937).

CA10. *Film Daily Year Book of Motion Pictures.* New York: 1918–70. Annual.

One of the earliest, and best, film directories. Detailed editorial index in front of volume. Although there is much more, separate sections give following information:
1. Statistics and financial summaries.
2. Film awards and best pictures of the year.
3. Full credits for feature films of previous year.
4. "Features Released since 1915," which gives titles (usually in English translation), distributors, and review date in *Film Daily* (New York, 1918–70). Last issues listed over 34,000 feature films.
5. "Original Titles," which names books and plays made into moving pictures with titles different from published version, giving original title, author, film title, and distributor. This also cumulates from 1915.
6. Film credits are cited for producers, authors, screenplay writers, music and art directors, cameramen, performers.
7. Personnel of studios, distributors, guilds, suppliers, newspaper correspondents.
8. Moving picture theaters and theater circuits in U.S. and Canada, by state and province.
9. Since late 1940s the *Year Book* included a comprehensive bibliography of books on film with general works, film arts and technology, biography and history, criticism, exhibitions, economic and legal aspects, society, film abroad, education, yearbooks, television.

Unfortunately, no longer published. Variously titled through the years: *Wid's Year Book, Film Year Book, Yearbook of Motion Pictures.* Final issue (1970): *Film TV Daily Yearbook of Motion Pictures and Television.*

CA11. *Film Review.* New York: 1944–. Annual.
Edited by F. Maurice Speed. Most useful section: "Releases of the Year in Detail." Abundantly illustrated; index to film titles.

CA12. *Guide to College Courses in Film and Television.* Washington, D.C.: Acropolis Books, 1973–.
Published for American Film Institute. 1975 edition describes 240 major programs and lists 791 schools that offer film and television courses. Gives courses, faculty, equipment, facilities, emphasis, plus a summary of purpose. Arranged by state. Lists schools by degree and schools with study courses for teachers; index to schools. Continues *Guide to College Film Courses* (Chicago: American Library Association, 1969–72). Paperback edition.

CA13. *International Film Guide.* South Brunswick and New York: A. S. Barnes and Co., Inc., 1964–. Annual.
Edited since 1964 by Peter Cowie. Most useful for "World Production Survey," which summarizes the year's developments by country; 1977 *Guide* surveys 42 countries. Sections on film festivals, film services, archives, schools, magazines (providing brief critiques of some film journals and outlining contents of important titles), book reviews, film book stores, etc.; essays written by film specialists. "Director of the Year" section briefly discusses five directors and provides a complete filmography of their work. Illustrated: indexed. Available in paperback.

CA14. *International Motion Picture Almanac.* New York: Quigley Publications, 1929–. Annual.
Currently edited by Richard Gertner. Almost half of each issue is a "Who's Who in Motion Pictures and Television." Other sections: statistics; feature pictures released during previous year (the 1970 issue gives 25-year cumulation; since 1971, *Almanac* covers "Feature Pictures: Jan. 1, 1955–"); corporations, including structure, organization, and executive personnel; theater circuits, both American and Canadian; drive-in theaters, by state; services; texts of codes and censorship; analyses of world market, by country. Useful section for research is "Publications on Motion Pictures," which includes: trade publications, newspapers, fan magazines, writers, and foreign correspondents. Detailed index of subjects.

Title varies: *The Motion Picture Almanac* (1929–35/36); *International Motion Picture Almanac* (1936/37–49/50); *Motion Picture and Television Almanac* (1951–55). Since 1956, published in two volumes as *International Motion Picture Almanac* and *International Television Almanac* (which repeats the "Who's Who" section). Edited 1933–49/50 by Terry Ramsaye; from 1950/51–70 by Charles S. Aaronson.

CA15. *Kemp's Film and Television Year Book (International).* London: Kemps Group/New York: International Publications Service, 1956–. Annual.

Also cited: *Kemp's Film and Television Directory.* Worldwide directory of agents, associations, services, laboratories, studios, etc., arranged in two sections. Part I covers Britain in full detail; preceded by indexes. Part II covers approximately thirty countries in varying detail (section for U.S. is extremely abbreviated). Each year varies somewhat—usually by expansion. First volume (1956) was titled: *Kemp's Short and Specialized Film and Independent Television Directory.*

CA16. *Motion Picture Market Place.* Boston: Little, Brown, 1976–.

Currently edited by Tom Costner. Subtitled: "The directory of production, professional talent, services and equipment for theatrical and television film." Covers 71 separate categories, from advertising agencies to wardrobe, with such sections as: literary and talent agents; distributors; festivals; equipment rental; film commissions; film libraries; major studios; music libraries; props; publications; special studios. Embraces entire U.S., all sections arranged by state and metropolitan area. Initiates a series planned for annual publication. Paperback edition.

CA17. Osborne, Robert. *Academy Awards Oscar Annual, 1971—.* La Habra, Calif.: ESE California.

In addition to Academy Awards, names nominees and winners of these annual awards: New York Film Critics, National Society of Film Critics, National Board of Review, Directors Guild, Writers Guild, Golden Globes, Image Award, Golden Apples, Harvard Lampoons, *New York Times, Los Angeles Times, Time Magazine,* British Academy Awards.

CA18. Perry, Ted, ed. *Performing Arts Resources.* New York: Drama Book Specialists, 1974—.

Sponsored by Theater Library Association and intended to be issued annually. Volume I (1974) describes these places for film research: special collections in New York; film resources in Los Angeles area; Film History Program of the Center for Advanced

Film Studies, American Film Institute; Motion Picture Section of Library of Congress; American Film Institute Catalog Project. Volume II (1975) includes guidelines for describing unpublished materials, by Eileen Bowser; and a bibliography of reference works for film study by Richard Dyer MacCann (originally published in February 1975 *Cinema Journal*). Volumes I and II will be indexed in Vol. III.

CA19. *La Produzione Italiana.* Rome: Unitalia Film, 1950–. Annual.

Catalog of new Italian films available for distribution. Each film accompanied by still and description in French, English, and Spanish (earlier volumes in Italian, French, and English). Gives literary source, basic credits, and cast. Directory of Italian distributors with addresses.

CA20. *Screen World.* New York: 1949–.

Also cited as *Daniel Blum's Screen World.* Edited since vol. 21 (1964/1965) by John Willis. Surveys films of the year. Casts and studio stills given for major pictures, both American and foreign. Only principals named for lesser films. Brief biographical data for film stars; full biographies given with obituary notices. Includes statistics, academy award winners. Index.

CA21. *TV Season.* Phoenix, Ariz.: Oryx Press, 1976–.

Currently edited by Nina David. Volumes now for 1974–75, 1975–76, and 1976–77. One of few sources for made-for-television movie casts and production credits. Describes the season's programs presented by national networks, including public television. All names indexed. Edition for 1973–74 is due.

CB. Directories

Directories are similar to annuals but are not published as regularly.

And they are diverse. Directories in this section provide a quick-reference source for awards, credits, and review dates, in the *New York Times Directory of the Film* (no. CB9); list libraries for film research, in *Performing Arts Libraries and Museums of the World* (no. CB4) and Rose's *World Film and Television Study Resources* (no. CB10); describe film festivals, in *Film and TV Festival Directory* (no. CB14); give sources for renting old films, in Muro's *Collecting and Enjoying Old Movies* (no. CB8); and much much more.

Check the Annuals (Section CA) for the same variety of information.

CB1. Beattie, Eleanor. *A Handbook of Canadian Film.* 2d ed. Toronto: Peter Martin Assoc./New York: N.Y. Zoetrope, 1976.
Directory of the Canadian film industry. More than half of volume lists living Canadian filmmakers, providing brief biography, complete filmography (when available), and bibliography. Other information: professional associations, film societies, study centers, film archives, trade journals and periodicals, directories, film catalogs, general publications (pertaining to Canadian film). Index to films mentioned. Available in paperback.

CB2. Chittock, John, ed. *World Directory of Stockshot and Film Production Libraries.* New York: Pergamon Press, 1969.
Published for International Film and Television Council. Lists 310 film production libraries and archives in 59 countries that can supply stockshot materials. (Stockshots may be extracts from newsreel or feature films, or footage taken for a film but never used; they may be single frames or extensive parts of complete films.) Printed in English and French; groups libraries by country. Some information given: library's specialization, date of oldest film preserved, whether library continues to acquire material, total amount of footage, rights of reproduction, restrictions. Paperback edition.

CB3. Emmens, Carol A., comp. *Film Resource Centers in New York City.* New York: Educational Film Library Association, 1976.
Lists 25 resource centers for film study in New York City. Describes services, facilities, and any special features. Pamphlet format.

Gottesman, R., and Geduld, H. M. *Guidebook to Film.* See no. A3.

CB4. International Federation of Library Associations. Section for Theatrical Libraries and Museums. *Performing Arts Libraries and Museums of the World.* André Veinstein, ed. 2d ed. Paris: Centre National de la Recherche Scientifique, 1967.
Also cited: *Bibliothéques et musées des arts du spectacle dans le monde.* Published in cooperation with UNESCO. Directory of libraries, museums, archives, special collections, etc., in 30 nations, arranged by French name. Within each country, libraries are grouped by city; for U.S., by state and city. Lists general characteristics, admission procedure, assistance given to reader, history

and nature of holdings, other activities (such as publications, exhibitions). Text in French and English. Index of names (cities, countries, individuals, institutions) and of separate collections. Consult subject index for these headings: cinema, films, motion pictures, television.

CB5. International Film and Television Council. *The I.F.T.C. Directory of International Film and Television Organizations and Their National Branches.* London: Film Centre Ltd., 1963.

Old now, but it provides information that can still be useful—addresses, films, publications. Index to names, organizations and countries.

CB6. McCallum, Heather. *Theater Resources in Canadian Collections. Research Collections in Canadian Libraries.* Ottawa: National Library of Canada, 1973.

Consult index for "Cinema collections" and "Film scripts."

CB7. Michael, Paul. *The Academy Awards. A Pictorial History.* 3d rev. ed. New York: Crown Publishers, 1975.

Photographic survey of the Oscar winners. Concentrates on performers and films, but lists all of the award winners. Arranged chronologically from first awards in 1927–28. Section of "losers" names unsuccessful nominees for best picture, actor, and actress. Can be updated by yearly almanacs, *Facts on File* (see no. IC12), and *Academy Awards Oscar Annual* (see no. CA17).

CB8. Muro, Fred F., Jr. *Collecting and Enjoying Old Movies.* Bellmore, N.Y.: Impact Promotion and Publishing, 1972.

Particularly useful as directory of sources for 8mm, super 8mm, and 16mm films, both silent and sound; dealers in posters, stills, and film-related memorabilia. Also describes over 100 classic silents made between 1914 and 1928, often noting the usual print quality.

Use with another guide for the film collector: *Collecting Classic Films* by Kalton C. Lahue (Garden City, N.Y.: American Photographic Book Publishing Co., 1970). Lists distributors of films and musical scores and discusses film, equipment, maintenance, sound.

CB9. *The New York Times Directory of the Film.* New York: Arno Press/Random House, 1971.

Practically the same volume as *Appendix/Index* for *New York Times Film Reviews* (see no. H7). Lists the *Times'* Ten Best Films of the Year, 1924–70; New York Film Critics' Circle Awards, 1935–70; Academy Awards, 1927–70; and reprints reviews of all these award-winning films. Other sections: portrait gallery of almost 2,000 movie stars; personal name index—which lists every performer, director, producer, screenwriter, etc. mentioned in *Times*' reviews, along with date of reviews, thereby providing a list of credits in chronological order; corporate index, to producing, distributing, and participating companies. (Of course, any film or filmmaker *not* mentioned in a review will not be included in this directory.) Covers 1913 through 1968. Introduction by Arthur Knight.

CB10. Rose, Ernest. *World Film and Television Study Resources.* Bonn-Bad Godesberg: Friedrich-Ebert-Stiftung, 1974. (Distributed in U.S. by University Film Association, Temple University, Philadelphia, Pa.)

Title continues: "A reference guide to major training centers and archives." Compiled in cooperation with University Film Association and International Liaison Center of Film and Television Schools.

Provides information on film and television schools and archives in 75 countries. Arranged by continent, then by country. For archives: gives holdings of films, stills, posters, books; information on screenings; other activities. For institutes: describes application procedures, program emphasis, special features, etc. Looseleaf format for planned revisions.

CB11. Special Libraries Association. Picture Division. *Picture Sources 3.* Edited by Ann Novotny. 3d ed. New York: Special Libraries Association, 1975.

Directory of picture collections in U.S. and Canada, grouped by type. Each entry gives address, director, nature and size of collection, subject strengths, restrictions. Check subject index for "motion picture industry and stills" and "actors and actresses"; nearly 50 sources named.

CB12. *World Communications: A 200-Country Survey of Press, Radio, Television, and Film.* 5th rev. ed. New York: Unipub/The Unesco Press, 1975.

Directory of communications facilities throughout the world, featuring film as well as press, radio, television. Arranged by continent, then by country. Gives these statistics (generally for 1971–72): films made; films imported and from what countries;

film theaters; seating capacity; annual attendance. Also describes the current situation in each country. Bibliography, pp. 529–33. The *Unesco Statistical Yearbook* can supplement and update this publication. Earlier editions were published by Unesco's Department of Mass Communications.

CB13. Young, William Curtis. *American Theatrical Arts; A Guide to Manuscripts and Special Collections in the United States and Canada.* Chicago: American Library Association, 1971.

Describes collections of manuscripts and other primary materials in 122 repositories in U.S. and Canada. Arranged by state or province. Includes collections of film scripts, patent records, papers of people involved with film, etc. Index to individuals; also lists film collections under "Motion Pictures."

CB14. Zwerdling, Shirley, ed. *Film & TV Festival Directory.* New York: Back Stage Publications, 1970.

Best source of information about the better-known film and television festivals. Lists American and international festivals, providing data necessary for filmmakers to enter their works in competitions. For U.S. names: award festivals, award presentations; amateur, independent, and academic film festivals; conventions, exhibits, and organizations. International festivals arranged by country. Cross-index of categories, and abbreviations. Geographical index.

Old now, but nothing else like it. *Motion Picture Market Place* (see no. CA16) lists current American film festivals. *International Film Guide* (no. CA13) and *Calendar of International Motion Picture and Television Events* (no. CA6) keep up with international festivals.

D. Bibliographies and Catalogs

A bibliography lists books on a particular subject. It might be used for finding what material exists on a topic; for ascertaining the basic or best books on a subject; for verifying incorrect or incomplete titles. A bibliography generally gives full information about each title and is arranged so that works can be found quickly by author or by subject. Most bibliographies are also indexed. This guide groups bibliographies as follows:

DA. Books on Moving Pictures: Comprehensive Bibliographies

Comprehensive bibliographies are complete in their listings of books up to a certain date. *The Film Index* (no. DA15), *General Bibliography of Motion Pictures* (no. DA14), and Rehrauer's *Cinema Booklist* and its supplements (nos. DA9 and DA10) are such collections and therefore important for any film research.

They may also be quite selective. Excellent examples of brief but thorough lists are Monaco and Schenker's *Books about Film* (no. DA7) and the bibliography in Robinson's *Man and the Movies* (DA11).

Several of the guides and handbooks (Section A) and the film histories (Section F) have useful bibliographies.

DA1. Blum, Eleanor. *Basic Books in the Mass Media*. Urbana: University of Illinois Press, 1972.

Subtitled: "An annotated, selected booklist covering general communications, book publishing, broadcasting, film, magazines, newspapers, advertising, indexes, and scholarly and professional periodicals." Section IV, "Film", describes 208 film books of all types: reference, general and national history, genre, yearbooks, etc. Arranged alphabetically by author. Restricted to English-language titles. Opening section, "General Communications," lists books that apply to three or more media. Subject and author-title indexes.

Bukalski, P. J. *Film Research: A Critical Bibliography.* . . . See no. A2.

Catalogo Bolaffi del cinema italiano. See nos. EB6 and EB7.

DA2. Christeson, Frances. *A Guide to the Literature of the Motion Picture.* Los Angeles: University of Southern California Press, 1938.

Bibliography of film books that were important in the late 1930s. Twenty-five essential works are thoroughly annotated, often giving full contents. Also lists film periodicals and 100 books that trace development of moving pictures. Subject index.

DA3. Cohen, Joan. "A Visual Explosion: The Growth of Film Literature," *Choice* 10 (March 1973): 26–40.

Bibliographical essay. Particularly recommended for these sections: Aesthetics, Theory and Language of Film; Criticism and Reviews; Genre Films; Published Screenplays.

Updates a similar list by Theodore Samore in February 1968 *Choice* (vol. 4, p. 1351–8). Includes individual biography and popular writing as well as standard works. Its eclectic scope makes it useful for the beginning student.

Enciclopedia dello spettacolo. See no. B6.

Film Daily Year Book of Motion Pictures. "Books on Filming." See no. CA10.

Filmlexicon degli autori e delle opere. See no. G4.

Garrett, G. P.; Hardison, O. B., and Gelfman, J. R. *Film Scripts.* See no. EE2.

Gessner, R. *The Moving Image: A Guide to Cinematic Literacy.* See no. FD6.

Gottesman, R., and Geduld, H. M. *Guidebook to Film: An Eleven-in-One Reference.* See no. A3.

Jacobs, L. *The Rise of the American Film.* See no. FB37.

Knight, A. *The Liveliest Art.* See no. FA7.

DA4. Kula, Sam. *Bibliography of Film Librarianship.* London: Library Association, 1967.

Cites general bibliographies, glossaries of terms, and references about storage, preservation, and copyright. Brief annotations. Author/title and subject indexes.

Manvell, R. *Film* and *The Film and the Public.* See nos. FA9 and FA10.

DA5. Manz, H. P., ed. *Internationale Filmbibliographie, 1952–1962.* Schweizerische Gesellschaft für Filmwissenschaft und Filmrecht. *Schriftenreihe,* Bd. 1 Zurich: Hans Rohr, 1963.

———. *Nachtrag, 1963–1964: 1965.* 2 vols. Zurich: 1964–65.

List reference books, film history, biography, technique, filmscripts, journals. Some entries annotated. Index.

DA6. Mitry, Jean, etab. *Bibliographie internationale du cinéma et de la télévision.* 3 vols. in 7. Paris: Institut des Hautes Études Cinématographiques, 1966–68/New York: International Publications Service, 1968. (In progress.)

When complete will cover film publications of Europe and U.S. Includes books and important journal articles; major works are annotated. Gives holdings of Paris libraries. So far: Part 1, by Mitry: France and French-language countries, in four volumes. Part 2, by Akakia Viala: Italy, in two volumes. Part 3, by Mitry: Spain, Portugal and Spanish- or Portuguese-language countries. Author index for each part. Other volumes planned for U.S.; England; Germany, Hungary, and German-language countries; Scandinavian countries; USSR, Poland, Czechoslovakia, Yugoslavia.

DA7. Monaco, James and Schenker, Susan. *Books about Film: A Bibliographical Checklist.* 3d ed. New York: New York Zoetrope, 1976.

A selective list of books that are generally available, particularly in paperback. Grouped by such topics as national cinemas, area studies, filmmakers, etc.; one unusual and important section is "New Criticism: Semiotics and Dialectics." Some entries are briefly described. Not indexed. Booklet format.

Monaco, J. *How to Read a Film.* Bibliography. See no. A7.

New York (City). Public Library. Research Libraries. *Catalog of the Theatre and Drama Collection. Part II. Theatre Collection: Books on the Theatre.* "Cinema" section. See no. DC4 and DC5.

Nicoll, A. *Film and Theatre.* See no. FD9.

DA8. Powers, Anne, comp. and ed. *Blacks in American Movies: A Selected Bibliography.* Metuchen, N.J.: Scarecrow Press, 1974.
Lists books, magazine and newspaper articles, and other materials on blacks in American films. Arrangement: nonperiodical references; periodical citations—by subject (then by periodical and by date); filmography of features, made between 1904 and 1930, by and about blacks. Limited to English-language items. Author and subject index.

DA9. Rehrauer, George. *Cinema Booklist.* Metuchen, N.J.: Scarecrow Press, 1972.
Describes and evaluates over 1,500 books devoted to film. Includes reference works, histories, scripts, biographies, criticism, etc. Arranged by *title* of book. Limited to English-language publications. Indexes: film scripts, authors, subjects.

DA10. ———. *Cinema Booklist Supplement, No. 1.* Metuchen, N.J.: Scarecrow Press, 1974.

———. *Cinema Booklist Supplement, No. 2.* 1977.
Supplement One describes books published during 1971 and 1972, with some early 1973 titles and items missed in first volumes—adding more than 900 entries. Supplement Two adds approximately 1,000 book titles, mainly published from 1973 to 1975. Both volumes cumulate indexes of previous edition: Film Script, Interview, Author, Subject. Future volumes are planned.

Reinert, C. *Kleines Filmlexikon.* See no. B19.

DA11. Robinson, William R., ed. *Man and the Movies.* With G. Garrett. Baton Rouge: Louisiana State University Press, 1967.
Notable here for its selective, critically annotated checklist of basic material, pp. 345–57, which includes comprehensive list of film periodicals. Bibliography prepared by George Broughton, Department of Radio, Television and Motion Pictures, University of North Carolina. Text consists of essays on film by well-known critics and writers. Available in paperback (Penguin Books, 1969).
Another excellent bibliography of film literature is included in I. C. Jarvie's *Movies and Society* (New York: Basic Books, 1970), pages 229–336. Arranged alphabetically by author; annotated.

DA12. Schoolcraft, Ralph Newman. *Performing Arts/Books in Print: An Annotated Bibliography.* New York: Drama Book Specialists, 1973.

Emphasizes theater, but includes film in Part 3: "Books on Motion Pictures, Television and Radio." Divided into two sections: books that were published prior to 1971, yet were still in print, and those which were published during 1971, as well as late additions. Arranged by broad topics—such as screenplays and individual biographies—each book is briefly described. List of publishers. Indexes: author and editor; title.

Continued by the quarterly *Annotated Bibliography of New Publications in the Performing Arts* (see no. DB1).

DA13. Turconi, Davide, and Bassotto, Camillo. *Il film e la sua storia (per una bibliografia delle storie del cinema)*. Venice: Cappelli editore, 1964.

Bibliography of histories of film, arranged by country of publication. Covers 30 countries. All entries are described, sometimes at length. Illustrated. Index to authors only.

DA14. Vincent, Carl; Redi, Riccardo; and Venturini, Franco. *Bibliografia generale del cinema/Bibliographie générale du cinéma/General Bibliography of Motion Pictures*. Rome: Edizioni dell-'Ateneo, 1953. (Reprinted: Arno Press, 1972.)

Compiled by Centro Cinematografico, University of Padua. Intended to be complete record of publications—books, articles, parts of books—concerning film up to 1953. All languages included, with Russian entries in Italian transliteration. Contents of more important books are summarized, but entries are not annotated. Works classified by broad topics: general, historiography, aesthetics and criticism, technique, etc. Classification scheme given at end. Preface in Italian, French, and English. Names indexed.

DA15. Writer's Program. New York. *The Film Index: A Bibliography. Volume I: The Film as Art*. Compiled by Writer's Program of the Work Projects Administration, City of New York. Edited by Harold Leonard. New York: 1941. (Reprinted: Arno Press, 1966.)

Part I, History and Technique, constitutes the most comprehensive bibliography of English-language books and articles published through 1935. About 8,600 entries, representing works of more than 2,000 authors, were drawn mostly from catalogs of Museum of Modern Art Library, New York Public Library, and Library of Congress. Arranged by broad subject areas; most entries are annotated. Many cross-references.

Part II lists films by type: fictional, factual, and miscellaneous. Every kind of genre included. Gives literary source, director, and major cast; cites reviews or criticism. Preface describes organization; table of contents serves as outline. Authors, titles of books and films, persons named in production credits, and major subjects are indexed. Projected volumes, to cover technological and sociological aspects, never published; information exists, however, on file cards in Museum of Modern Art Library.

DB. Books on Moving Pictures: Continuing Bibliographies

Continuing bibliographies record the literature on a regular basis, usually every year, and thereby update older lists. In some cases, such as the *Annotated Bibliography of New Publications in the Performing Arts* (no. DB1), they continue a basic work (Schoolcraft's *Performing Arts/Books in Print;* no. DA12), providing a continuous record of the literature of the subject.

Almost every library will have the *Cumulative Book Index* (no. DE10) and the *Subject Guide to Books in Print* (no. DB6). Together, these general sources can update any list of books.

The *Bibliographie internationale cinéma* (no. DB3) may not be easy to locate, but it can save a great deal of work for anyone requiring foreign publications—as well as English-language books.

DB1. *Annotated Bibliography of New Publications in the Performing Arts.* New York: Drama Book Specialists, No. 8&9, 1972–. Quarterly.

Continues Schoolcraft's *Performing Arts/Books in Print* (see no. DA12) (with issue no. 8 & 9, 1972). Identical format. Consult Part Three: "Books on Motion Pictures, Television and Radio."

Annuaire du cinéma et télévision. See no. CA1.

DB2. *Bibliographic Index: A Cumulative Bibliography of Bibliographies.* New York: H. W. Wilson Co., 1937–. Semiannual.

Subject index to separately published bibliographies and to bibliographies printed within books, periodicals, reports. Entries under "Moving Pictures" cover all aspects: industry, sound, studios and theaters, amateur film, etc. Cross-references. Foreign-language publications included. Cumulates annually.

DB3. *Bibliographie internationale cinéma.* Bucharest: Arhiva Nationala de Filme, 1966–. Annual.

Project of Fédération Internationale des Archives du Film (FIAF). Bibliography of publications about film, printed in Rumanian and French. Arranged by broad subject areas such as reference sources; theory and aesthetics; film history, with national film histories arranged by country. Biography section arranged by directors, screenwriters, performers, and so on. Indexes: names (including authors and subjects), titles, country of origin, publishing house. Runs about two years late.

DB4. British Film Institute. Information and Documentation. *Book Library Bibliography.* London: British Film Institute (not dated—since 1960s?).

Selected bibliographies on individuals and subjects. Cites relevant books, periodical articles, chapters in books, pamphlets. Includes foreign language materials. Leaflet format.

Cumulative Book Index. See no. DE10.

DB5. *Essay and General Literature Index.* New York: H. W. Wilson, Co., 1900–.

Indexes essays and critical articles published in collections and anthologies. Authors and subjects arranged in one alphabet. Material on individuals entered under name. Also consult "Moving Pictures" and its subdivisions. Semiannual with annual cumulations.

Film Daily Year Book of Motion Pictures. "Books on Filming." See no. CA10.

Film Quarterly. See no. IA6.

International Motion Picture Almanac. See no. CA14.

DB6. *Subject Guide to Books in Print, An Index to the Publishers' Trade List Annual.* New York: R. R. Bowker, 1957–. Annual.

A source of current film books. Consult such subject headings as "Moving Picture Actors and Actresses," "Moving Picture Criticism," "Moving Picture Plays," "Moving Pictures" (for general works) and its many subdivisions. Updated by *Forthcoming Books* (bimonthly) and its *Subject Guide.*

DC. Books on Moving Pictures: Catalogs

Catalogs specify the books in a particular collection. They, too, may be used to suggest titles for film research. In addition, they describe the holdings of libraries that might be visited or contacted. Catalogs of the Theater Collection of the New York Public Library (no. DC4), University of California at Los Angeles (no. DC3), and the British Film Institute (no. DC1) collections can all serve this dual purpose.

DC1. British Film Institute. *Catalogue of the Book Library of the British Film Institute.* 3 vols. Boston: G. K. Hall, 1975.

The BFI Library in London is one of the best in the world. It comprises over 20,000 books in many languages, early catalogs of films and film apparatus, and over 4,000 film scripts (mostly British and American films plus English dialogue scripts for many foreign films shown at National Film Theatre).

Arrangement: author catalog; title catalog; script catalog, including screenplays, shooting scripts, translations, published scripts, analytical entries for script collections; subject catalog, which is divided into three sections: Personality Index, arranged alphabetically by name; Film Index, which cites criticism, production diaries, etc. of individual films, arranged by title; book collection, arranged by BFI Classification (based on Dewey Decimal System). Vol. III concludes with an alphabetical index to this section, which refers to BFI Classification number (warning: this part is not easy to use).

Catalog excludes periodicals (see no. IB1). Format: photographic reproduction of catalog cards themselves.

DC2. International Federation of Film Archives. *Catalogue collectif des livres et périodiques publiés avant 1914* ... Brussels: Cinémathèque Royale de Belgique, 1967.

Titled in English: *Union Catalogue of Books and Periodicals Published before 1914.* Chronological listing of books and periodicals related to prehistory and early history of film, covering 1646–1914. Broad in scope: includes works on physics and optics, manufacturers' catalogs, etc. Based on collections in Federation (FIAF); institution reporting each entry is given. Author and title indexes in front of volume.

DC3. *Motion Pictures: A Catalog of Books, Periodicals, Screen Plays and Production Stills.* Theatre Arts Library, University of California at Los Angeles. 2d ed., rev. and exp. Boston: G. K. Hall, 1976.

Compiled by Audree Malkin. Catalog is arranged in five sections: books, periodicals, and journals; published screenplays; unpublished screenplays; television scripts; and production stills.

The book/periodical collection includes the historical, critical, aesthetic, biographical, and technical aspects of film. Books are entered by author only. Format is a photographic reproduction of card catalog. Excluded from the catalog are clippings, film festival programs, film distribution catalogs, and portraits of personalities, although these are included in the UCLA collection.

The information in this catalog can be supplemented and expanded by another catalog that is in preparation: *Motion Pictures, Television and Radio: A Union Catalogue of Manuscript and Special Collections in the Western United States.* Compiled and edited by Linda Mehr. Sponsored by the Film and Television Study Center, Inc. Anne G. Schlosser, Project Director. (Boston: G. K. Hall, 1977).

DC4. New York (City). Public Library, Research Libraries. *Catalog of the Theatre and Drama Collections. Part II: Theatre Collection: Books on the Theatre.* 9 vols. Boston: G. K. Hall, 1967.

Photographic reproduction of card catalog of New York Public Library Theater Collection. Includes books, periodicals, important articles, microfilms, dissertations; contains more than 23,500 items. Authors, subjects, titles arranged in one alphabet. "Theater" embraces moving pictures, radio, and television as well as most other entertainments. Titles grouped under "Cinema" and its subdivisions constitute one of the most complete bibliographies of world film up to 1967. These subdivisions are especially rich: catalogs, directories and yearbooks, history and criticism, periodicals (by locality), printed texts and outlines. Approximately 1,900 scripts listed by title under "Cinema—Scripts": includes manuscripts, shooting scripts for moving pictures and radio, television production scripts. Geographical subdivisions, Africa to Yugoslavia. Theater Collection also includes ephemera such as clippings, photographs, prints, manuscripts, scrapbooks, and the like that are not listed in catalog.

DC5. ———. *Supplement. Part II. Theatre Collection: Books on the Theatre.* Boston: 1973.

Continues above, through 31 December 1971. Beginning January 1972, all additions to the theater collections are included in the *Dictionary Catalog of the Research Libraries.* (Issued as basic volumes with monthly cumulative supplements.)

DC6. *Book Store Catalogs.*

Several book stores specialize in moving-picture materials and print catalogs of books, periodicals, and so on that are available for sale. They include out-of-print items. Write directly for information.

Cinemabilia, 10 West 13th St., New York, N.Y. 10011

Drama Bookshop, 150 West 52d St., New York, N.Y. 10019

Gotham Book Mart and Gallery, 41 West 47th St., New York, N.Y. 10036

Hampton Books, Route 1, Box 76, Newberry, South Carolina 29108

Larry Edmunds Bookshop, 6658 Hollywood Blvd., Hollywood, Calif. 90028

Limelight Bookstore, 1803 Market St., San Francisco, Calif. 94103

Cine Books, 692a Yonge Street, Toronto, Ontario, Canada

DD. Book Reviews

The following indexes can locate reviews of books about moving pictures. *Book Review Digest* (no. DD1) usually extracts enough of a review that one can form an idea of the book.

Batty, L. *Retrospective Index to Film Periodicals.* See no. IC1.

DD1. *Book Review Digest.* New York: H. W. Wilson, 1905–. Monthly.

Either digests or cites reviews printed in approximately 70 major periodicals and some newspaper supplements. Arranged by author of book reviewed, with subject and title indexes. Limited to books published or distributed in U.S. Nonfiction must be reviewed in two places to be included. Annual cumulations.

DD2. *Book Review Index.* Detroit: Gale Research Co., 1965–.

Cites reviews of humanities- and social sciences-oriented books in more than 200 journals. The sources are usually more scholarly than those in *Book Review Digest,* above. Arrangement is by author of books reviewed.

Bowles, S. E. *Index to Critical Film Reviews in British and American Film Periodicals.* See no. H2.

Film Literature Index. See no. IC3.

DE. National Bibliographies

National bibliographies attempt to list everything published in a particular country during a stated period of time. Most are arranged by author, therefore books on moving pictures cannot be located by subject. They are generally useful in verifying citations.

Countries included:
England
France
Germany
Italy
United States

In addition, the *National Union Catalog* (no. DE9) lists the major libraries in the United States that have each book. This can be a boon to anyone doing research in a small library. For when the local library does not have a particular book it is possible to request it through the *interlibrary loan* department. This is a system by which one library can borrow books (and sometimes journals) from another library for its users.

Interlibrary loan is a regular service in all libraries, but one disadvantage is that it may take several weeks to receive the book. One should consider this when establishing a timetable for a research project.

England

DE1. British Museum. *General Catalogue of Printed Books.* 263 vols. London: 1931–66.

───. ───. *Ten-Year Supplement, 1956–1965.* 50 vols. London: 1968.

───. ───. *Five-Year Supplement, 1966–1970.* London: 1971–72.

Catalog of printed books in Library of British Museum dating from 15th century through 1970, in all languages except Oriental. In addition to possessing collections in all fields and languages, the British Museum is England's copyright depository, its *Catalogue* is therefore the most comprehensive collection of British publications. Author catalog only with some cross-references (e.g., under personal names, biographical and critical works are cited). Often analyzes series. Can be continued by:

DE2. *British National Bibliography.* London: 1950–.
Based on accessions by British Museum, this weekly bibliography is arranged in classified order. Weekly and monthly indexes of authors, titles, subjects. Cumulated into annual and quinquennial volumes.

France

DE3. *Bibliographie de la France.* Paris: 1811–.
Standard weekly list of material received through legal deposit. Three main parts: Part 1 is the bibliography, with subsections for periodicals and dissertations. Part 3 includes indexes to Part 1. Cumulated annually.

Germany

DE4. *Deutsche Bibliographie.* Frankfurt, a.M.: 1947–.
Lists German-language books, regardless of country of publication. Cumulations arranged by title with keyword and subject index. Weekly (*Wöchentliches Verzeichnis*); cumulates semiannually (*Halbjahres*) and quinquenially (*Fünfjahres*). The national bibliography for West Germany.

DE5. *Deutsche Nationalbibliographie.* Leipzig: 1931–.
Bibliography arranged in two sections: Part A, weekly, trade books; Part B, semimonthly, publications such as dissertations and society proceedings. Both sections in classified order with author and keyword-title indexes. Includes periodicals. The national bibliography for East Germany.

Italy

DE6. Florence. Biblioteca Nazionale Centrale. *Catalogo cumulativo 1886–1957 del Bollettino delle pubblicazioni italiane ricevute per diritto di stampa dalla biblioteca....* 39 vols. Nendeln, Liechtenstein: 1968.
Cumulates 72 volumes of the *Bollettino,* issued monthly between 1886 and 1957 by the National Library of Florence. The *Bollettino,* based on copyright deposit, was the most complete record of Italian publications for the period of its existence. Lists authors, anonymous works, and serial titles in one alphabet. Can be continued by:

DE7. *Bibliografia nazionale italiana; nuova serie del Bollettino delle pubblicazioni italiane ricevute per diritto di stampa.* Florence: 1958–.

A current record of books and pamphlets received by legal deposit. Author-title index in each issue.

Monthly. Separate annual index lists all main entries in one alphabet. Includes index to subjects.

United States

DE8. U.S. Library of Congress. *Catalog of the Books Represented by Library of Congress Printed Cards Issued to July 31, 1942.* 167 vols. Washington, D.C.: 1942–46.

———. ———. *Supplement, 1942–1947.* 42 vols. Washington, D.C.: 1948.

———. ———. *Supplement, 1948–1952.* 24 vols. Washington, D.C.: 1953.

Photographic reproduction of cards, printed by the Library of Congress, representing books added to its collection from 1898 to mid-1942. Two supplements include accessions from 1942 through 1952. Subsequent accessions are incorporated in:

DE9. *The National Union Catalog: A Cumulative Author List.* Washington, D.C.: U.S. Library of Congress, 1956–.

Cited as *NUC*. Represents holdings of Library of Congress and over 800 large American libraries. Lists books and other publications by author, with cross-references where necessary. Issued in nine monthly issues with quarterly and annual cumulations. Subject catalogs are also available for the period 1950 onward.

DE10. *Cumulative Book Index.* New York: H. W. Wilson, 1898–.

Cited as *CBI*. The most complete record of American publications, from 1898 to date, with full bibliographic data. Since 1928, has included publications from rest of English-speaking world. Lists authors, titles, and subjects in one alphabet. Monthly; cumulates annually and later into multiannual volumes.

E. Film Lists and Sources

A film list is often called a filmography, based on the word for a list of books—bibliography. Along with the film's title, filmographies generally provide such information as director, cast, production date or year of release, country of origin, running time, and perhaps a story summary.

Many of the film histories (Section F) include lists of important or representative films; and film periodicals (Section I) often publish filmographies.

EA. International Filmographies

International filmographies list films of many countries. The most comprehensive of all is the British Film Institute's *Film Title Index* (no. EA2), which lists 200,000 films. But because it is so expensive, it will not be widely available.

The most useful international filmographies for students in this country will probably be "Features Released since 1915" in the *Film Daily Year Book* (no. CA10), index of the *World Encyclopedia of the Film* (no. G17), Limbacher's *Feature Films on 8mm and 16mm* (no. ED8), or *TV Feature Film Source Book* (no. ED12).

The following filmographies are also important.

EA1. Baer, D. Richard, ed. *The Film Buff's Bible of Motion Pictures (1915–1972).* Hollywood: Hollywood Film Archive, 1972.

Appraises some 13,000 moving pictures, released through September 1972, that are likely to appear on television. Arranged by film title; includes silent films, short features, foreign-made films, films made for television. Gives year released, running time, distributor. Index of alternate titles. Available in paperback. A revised edition is due in 1978.

EA2. British Film Institute. *Film Title Index, 1908–1974.* London: World Microfilms Publications, 1976(?).

Microfilm (120 reels) of British Film Institute's card index to 200,000 films produced throughout the world. Includes feature films, documentaries, and cartoons. Gives production credits, brief synopsis, cites reviews and articles. Arranged alphabetically by original title with cross-references. A biennial supplement is planned to cover new cards. Also includes index to journal *Bioscope*, 1908–1932. Unfortunately, a printed index does not accompany this set. The National Film Archive *Catalogue* (see no. EA8) can suggest silent films that are included.

EA3. Charensol, Georges. *Le cinéma.* Paris: Librarie Larousse, 1966.

Important for "Filmographie," which charts the world's principal films from 1895 through 1965, by year and country. Gives, in tabular form: director, film title in French and original language, scenarist, origin of work, cameramen, composer, scene designer, main cast. Table of contents at back. Index to film titles and names.

EA4. Cowie, Peter, gen. ed. *World Filmography 1967.* South Brunswick and New York: A. S. Barnes and Co., Inc., 1977.

Gives full credits for feature films made in 45 countries during 1967. Arranged by country, by original title. Briefly describes many of the films. Inclusion is based on first theatrical release in the country of origin during 1967. Crossreferences for co-productions. Illustrated with stills. Indexes to alternative and translated titles and to directors. Future volumes planned to go backwards in time, to the end of the 19th century, and to move forward to the present. *World Filmography 1968* is due in late 1977.

EA5. Cyr, Helen W. *A Filmography of the Third World: An Annotated List of 16mm Films.* Metuchen, N.J.: Scarecrow Press, 1976.

Includes all non-Western nations and the ethnic minorities of North America and Europe. Lists short and feature-length films, fact and fictional. Majority of films were released in 1960s and 1970s, but also includes older films. Films are briefly described, with this information given for feature-length theatrical films: language; English-language subtitles, if any; credits for screenplay, music, photography, production, cast. All films are available for distribution in U.S. or Canada. Directory of film distributors. List of directors, cinematographers, scenarists, and composers, with their films. Index to film titles.

Enciclopedia dello spettacolo. Indice-repertorio. See no. B9.

EA6. Esnault, Philippe. *Chronologie du cinéma mondial des origines à nos jours.* Paris: Les Grand Films Classiques, 1963.
 Chronology of technical developments and important films, from beginnings to 1961. Arranged by date, country, and director. Name index.

Film Daily Year Book of Motion Pictures. "Features Released since 1915." See no. CA10.

EA7. Fox, Stuart, comp. *Jewish Films in the United States: A Comprehensive Survey and Descriptive Filmography.* Boston: G. K. Hall, 1976.
 Sponsored by the A. F. Rad Jewish Film Archives. Filmography of films concerned with Jews and Judaism, listing films made in U.S. and those released or distributed in U.S. Includes features, shorts, documentaries, newsreels, television productions, etc. Most entries are briefly described. Indexes to film titles and to subjects.

The International Encyclopedia of Film. Index. See no. B13.

Limbacher, J. L. *Feature Films on 8mm and 16mm.* See no. ED8.

EA8. London. National Film Archive. *Catalogue.* 3 vols. London: British Film Institute/New York: International Publications Service, 1960–66. (In progress.)
 Part I: *Silent News Films, 1895–1933* (1st ed., 1951. Also known as *National Film Library Catalogue*). Part II: *Silent Non-Fiction Films, 1895–1934.* Part III: *Silent Fiction Films, 1895–1930.*
 Catalog of silent films available at the British Film Institute. Since the Institute's collection includes films from approximately twenty filmmaking nations, this is the first attempt at a comprehensive published list of the world's films. Catalog of sound films to be published later. Arrangement varies:
 Part I, *Silent News Films:* arranged by year. Gives name of event, date of event or of film's issue, producer (when known), brief description, footage. Detailed index lists names and events in one alphabet. Emphasis on British news events, but films from other countries are included.
 Part II, *Silent Non-Fiction Films:* arranged by country, then year. Gives title, producer, director, editors, etc.; brief description; footage. Indexes: film titles and subjects.
 Part III, *Silent Fiction Films:* arranged by country, then year. Gives title; credits (when known); summary of story; footage.

Contains about 2,000 titles; 773 are American, 555 British. Index of film titles and names.

EA9. Mitry, Jean. *Filmographie universelle.* 11 vols. Paris: Institut des Hautes Études Cinématographiques, 1963–69. (In progress.)

Projected as a universal filmography. Arranged by *école* (either producing company or country), then by director. For each gives brief biography and chronological record of films; full credits listed when known. Vol. 1 outlines the plan for entire series. Table of contents in each volume; no indexes so far.

To date, series covers: vol. 1: technical developments from 1860 through 1962; vol. 2: earliest filmmakers of France and Europe, 1895–1912, arranged by producing company; vols. 3 and 4: earliest filmmakers of U.S., 1895–1915, arranged by producing company; vol. 4 includes film serials, 1912 through 1920; vol. 5: Italy, Denmark, Sweden, 1910–25; vols. 6–11: American filmmakers, 1910–25.

Muro, F. F. *Collecting and Enjoying Old Movies.* See no CB8.

EA10. Niver, Kemp R. *Motion Pictures from the Library of Congress Paper Print Collection, 1894–1912.* Berkeley: University of California Press, 1967.

Indexes films released in U.S. between 1894 and 1912 that were deposited on reels of photographic paper for copyright. Most were produced in America, but some in France, Britain, and Scandinavia. About 3,000 prints are described and grouped by type. Credits given as fully as possible, along with condition, synopsis, and interesting technical features. Entries based on what was actually viewed by compilers and therefore constitute a primary source for the first eighteen years of filmmaking. Performers, directors, and cameramen were seldom given credit for their work, but they are named when this could be determined. Griffith, Ince, Porter/Edison and Sennett films are indexed under Director heading. Detailed subject index; title index. Copies (16 mm celluloid) of prints in this collection may be purchased from the Library of Congress.

Pickard, R. A. E. *Dictionary of 1,000 Best Films.* See no. EG5.

EA11. Sadoul, Georges. *Dictionary of Films.* Translated, edited, and updated by Peter Morris. Berkeley: University of California Press, 1972.

Lists films alphabetically under original-language title with cross-references from all known release titles. International in scope, although emphasis is on European films; includes silent and sound films. Gives credits, plot outline, and critical comments by this famous film scholar. Illustrated. Expands the original *Dictionnaire des films* (Paris: Éd. du Seuil, 1967) by some 15 percent, adding films not in that volume, but does not include its index to directors and critics. Nor is there cross-referencing between this volume and its companion, *Dictionary of Film Makers* (see no. G13). Available in paperback.

Sarris, A. *The American Cinema*. Directorial Index. See no. EC10.

Screen World. See no. CA20.

Smith, J. M. and Cawkwell, T. *World Encyclopedia of the Film*. Index. See no. G17.

TV Feature Film Source Book. See no. ED12.

Writer's Program. New York. *The Film Index*. See no. DA15.

EB. National Filmographies

National filmographies list the films of individual countries. The following selection is far from complete, but most of the books are generally available.

Countries included:
<table>
<tr><td>Africa</td><td>Germany</td></tr>
<tr><td>Canada</td><td>Italy</td></tr>
<tr><td>China</td><td>Japan</td></tr>
<tr><td>Eastern Europe</td><td>Soviet Union</td></tr>
<tr><td>England</td><td>Sweden</td></tr>
<tr><td>France</td><td>United States</td></tr>
</table>

An excellent source for research in this area, although unfortunately it will not be found in many libraries, is:

EB1. *Répertoire mondial des filmographies nationales*. Ervin Voiculescu. Bucharest: Archiva Nationala de Filme, 1970.

Cites national film lists for 44 countries. Thorough listing; booklet format.

Africa

Les cinéma africains en 1972. See no. FB1.

Canada

EB2. Morris, Peter, ed. *Canadian Feature Films: 1913–1969.* 3 vols. Ottawa: Canadian Film Institute, 1970–76.
Use for information prior to *Film Canadiana* (see no. CA8). Provides detailed filmographies that give production credits, synopses, notes on production, extracts from reviews for indigenous films and films shot in Canada. Films are arranged by date. Indexes to personalities and titles.

China

Leyda, J. *Dianying: An Account of Films and the Film Audience in China.* See no. FB2.

Eastern Europe

Hibbin, N. *Eastern Europe: An Illustrated Guide.* See no. FB3.

Nemeskúrty, I. *Word and Image: History of the Hungarian Cinema.* See no. FB5.

Stoil, M. J. *Cinema Beyond the Danube.* See no. FB6.

England

British Film and Television Year Book. See no. CA5.

Durgnat, R. *A Mirror for England: British Movies from Austerity to Affluence.* See no. FB7.

Gifford, D. *British Cinema.* See no. FB8.

EB3. Gifford, Denis. *The British Film Catalog, 1895–1970: A Reference Guide.* 2 vols. New York: McGraw-Hill, 1973.
Vol. 1: Silent Films; vol. 2: Sound Films. Chronological guide to all British feature films made between 1895 and 1970—nearly 15,000 titles. Information given: studio, release date, running time, director, cast, brief description of film, story source. Also includes American-British co-productions. Bibliography. Index to film titles.

London. National Film Archive. *Catalogue.* See no. EA8.

France

Annuaire du cinéma et télévision. See no. CA1.

Annuaire du spèctacle: cinéma. . . . See no. CA2.

EB4. *Index de la cinématographie française.* 18 vols. Paris: 1947–65. Annual.
Supplement to weekly *Cinématographie française, la Revue des professionels du cinéma.* Index summarizes films shown in France during previous year. Gives producer, cast, genre, brief synopsis and analysis, and title in original language; arranged by French title. Short films analyzed separately. Cumulative directories of performers (*vedettes*) and directors (*réalisateurs*), both French and foreign, list their films and refer to issues where each was discussed. Film titles cumulating from the first volume are indexed. Format changes from volume to volume. Ceased publication after 1965 when *Cinématographie française* changed editors and name to *Film français.*

Sadoul, G. *Le cinéma français.* See no. FB14.

Germany

EB5. Bauer, Alfred. *Deutscher Spielfilm Almanach, 1929–1950.* Berlin: Filmblätter Verlag, 1951. (Reprint: Munich: Filmladen Christoph Winterberg, 1976.)
Chronological listing of sound films produced in Germany, with production credits. Index to film titles. Reprint adds an index to names.
Note: Filmographies for East and West Germany are numerous and complex; see *Répertoire mondial des filmographies nationales* (no. EB1) for comprehensive listing.

Italy

Annuario del cinema italiano. See no. CA3.

EB6. *Catalogo Bolaffi del cinema italiano. Tutti i film italiani dopoguerra.* Gianni Rondolino, dir. Turin: G. Bolaffi, 1967.
Covers twenty years of Italian film, 1945 through 1965. Films arranged chronologically by year, then alphabetically by title. Gives: genre, director, principal performers, producers, box-

office receipts. Annotated bibliography of books published during this period. Index to film titles. Table of contents at back. Updated by:

EB7. *Catalogo Bolaffi del cinema italiano 1966/1975: tutti i film degli ultimi 10 anni.* A cura di Gianni Rondolino. Turin: Bolaffi, 1975.
  Updates original volume, above, through 1975. Identical format.

Leprohon, P. *The Italian Cinema.* See no. FB21.

EB8. Lizzani, Carlo. *Storia del cinema italiano, 1895–1961.* Florence: Parenti, 1961.
  Important for Appendix "Film a soggetto," with filmographies of 58 Italian directors through 1960 (providing literary source, credits, cast; directors arranged alphabetically, films listed chronologically); and list of documentaries, by directors. Illustrated with film stills; illustrations are indexed but not text. The principal history of early Italian film.

EB9. Savio, Francesco. *Ma L'Amore No; realismo, formalismo, propaganda e telefoni bianchi nel cinema italiano di regime (1930–1943).* Milan: Sonzogno, 1975.
  Catalog of films made in Italy during the Fascist period. Gives credits, plot, critical comments, brief bibliography, alternate titles. Separate section of unfinished works. Illustrated with film stills.

Japan

Svensson, A. *Japan.* See no. FB26.

Soviet Union

Birkos, A. S. *Soviet Cinema: Directors and Films.* See no. FB31.

Leyda, J. *Kino: A History of the Russian and Soviet Film.* See no. FB32.

EB10. *Catalogue of Soviet Feature Films.* Moscow: Sovexportfilm, 1958.
  Catalog of Soviet films available from distributor, Sovexportfilm. Printed in Russian, French, Spanish, and English. Gives this information: studio, year of release, screenwriter, director,

cameraman, art director, composer, sound director, principal characters, brief synopsis of each film. Illustrated with stills. Arranged by Russian title, with indexes for other languages.

Sweden

Cowie, P. *Sweden*. See no. FB27.

United States

EB11. American Film Institute. *The American Film Institute Catalog of Motion Pictures Produced in the United States.* Kenneth W. Munden, ed. New York: R. R. Bowker, 1971–. (In progress.)

So far: *Feature Films, 1921–1930* (1971: 1 vol. in 2) and *Feature Films, 1961–1970* (1976: 1 vol. in 2). When complete, will be the most thorough filmography of American film. Master plan is to fill 19 volumes, covering: film beginnings, 1893–1919, in one volume; feature films 1911–70, six volumes; short films, 1911–70, six volumes; newsreels, 1908–70, six volumes. *Feature Films* series will list every performer, writer, director, assistant. Two volumes published to date: films released between 1921 and 1930, produced by American studios, societies, institutions, etc.; films released between 1961 and 1970, including foreign films released in U.S. The AFI is currently working on the teens.

Films are listed alphabetically by U.S. release title with cross-references from variant titles. Gives: physical description; production and cast credits; summary; source of story idea. Separate volume includes credit and subject indexes. Credit index has two parts: (1) personal and corporate names in one alphabet, giving productions by year; (2) literary and dramatic source, arranged alphabetically by author. Title given is always that of the film; source is given in the catalog proper (e.g., index volume gives Balzac literary credit for 1921 film *The Conquering Power;* catalog entry names original source: *Eugenie Grandet*).

Subject Index identifies films by detailed list of descriptors, including characterizations, themes, dates and seasons, historical events, places and geographical features, people, cinematic devices, etc. Introduction to each section should be read with care.

Film Daily Year Book of Motion Pictures. "Features Released since 1915." See no. CA10.

EB12. *Film Notes.* New York: Museum of Modern Art, 1969.

On title page: "Chronological Annotated List of American Fiction Films Produced Between 1894–1950. . . ." Films arranged by such topics as: "Films of the 1890's," "Three Vitagraph Comedies," "Musicals of the Thirties," giving date, running time, producing company, full credits. Preface states that notes for each film are "tentative and incomplete; they waver between information and comment." They often relate a film to other works of the same director or genre. Brief bibliography. Indexes to filmmakers and film titles. Updates *Film Notes* produced by Museum of Modern Art in 1935 and 1949.

EB13. Lauritzen, Einar, and Lundquist, Gunnar. *American Film-Index 1908–1915.* Stockholm, Sweden: Film Index/Akademibokhandeln, 1976.

Subtitled: "23,000 Titles from the Forgotten Years of the American Film." Starts with first film directed by D. W. Griffith, in July 1908, and continues through 1915. Arranged alphabetically by title; refers to issue of *Moving Picture World* for story plot (thereby serving as an index to *MPW*); gives date, producing company, director, cast (when known). Excludes pictures shorter then 390 ft., except for productions of American Biograph (in order to include all Griffith films). Does not include documentaries or newsreels.

Provides brief histories of 135 film companies of the period. Illustrated with full-page portraits of performers and directors.

Michael, P. *The American Movies Reference Book.* See no. B14.

EB14. U.S. Copyright Office. *Motion Pictures 1894–1912 Identified from the Records of the U.S. Copyright Office,* by Howard Lamarr Walls. Washington, D.C.: U.S. Library of Congress, 1953.

Catalog of 8,506 works copyrighted between 1894 and 1912. First part lists films alphabetically by title. Each entry gives title, name of copyright claimant (generally the producer), date of copyright, and registration number. Second part is claimant index. Under each claimant, moving picture titles are arranged chronologically, making this an inventory of American film-company productions for each year. Precedes *Cumulative Series* (see below). Niver's *Motion Pictures from the Library of Congress Paper Print Collection* (see no. EA10), describes about 3,000 of the films listed in this catalog.

EB15. U.S. Copyright Office. *Motion Pictures. Catalog of Copyright*

Entries, Cumulative Series. Washington, D.C.: U.S. Library of Congress, 1951–.
Motion Pictures 1912–1939.
Motion Pictures 1940–1949.
Motion Pictures 1950–1959.
Motion Pictures 1960–1969.
Each volume lists films registered for copyright during the stated period. Consists of three parts: first section lists films by title, giving claimant, copyright date, and registration number; also provides—when available—translated or alternate title, series title, production statement, physical description, literary source of story, production credits, author of film story. Cross-references for alternate and translated titles. Second section indexes persons and organizations responsible for productions and lists authors of story source; credits given for each person indexed. Third section indexes series titles.

Format for *Motion Pictures 1960–1969* is somewhat different. Main entry no longer provides production credits, and series titles are included with film titles. Contains television commercials, series, and news stories. Continued by semiannual supplement. Can be augmented and updated by nos. EB16 and EB17, below.

Note: Together, nos. EB14 and EB15 provide an unbroken record of copyright registration of moving pictures in U.S. It is not complete, however, because some films were never submitted for copyright.

EB16. U.S. Library of Congress. *Library of Congress Catalog.* Washington, D.C.: U.S. Library of Congress, 1953–. (Also available in reprint editions)

Author Catalog, 1948–1952. Vol. 24, Films. (Began including film in 1951. Not indexed.)

National Union Catalog, 1953–1957. Vol. 28, Motion Pictures and Filmstrips.

Author Catalog, 1958–1962. Vols. 53–54, Motion Pictures and Filmstrips.

National Union Catalog, 1963–1967. Vols. 71–72, Motion Pictures and Filmstrips.

National Union Catalog, 1968–1972. Motion Pictures and Filmstrips.

These volumes reproduce the catalog cards for motion pictures and filmstrips printed by the Library of Congress during each period. Emphasis is on films of educational or instructive nature, released in U.S. or Canada, but also include theatrical motion pictures. The subject index groups them together under that heading; also check "Musical Revues, Comedies" and similar headings. Films are entered by title with this information: technical data, producer and producing company, author, literary source, director and cast for theatrical films, brief plot summary. Quinquennial. Superseded by:

EB17. U.S. Library of Congress. *Films and Other Materials for Projection.* Washington, D.C.: 1973–.

Continues *Motion Pictures and Filmstrips*, above. Now includes sets of slides and of transparencies, as well as moving pictures and filmstrips. Limited to material of educational and instructional value released in U.S. and Canada. Provides brief summary of most films. Lists producers and distributors of currently available materials. Quarterly.

Note: From 1951 through April 1957 cards were printed by the Library of Congress for virtually all motion pictures and filmstrips that were registered for copyright. Since May 1957 cards have been printed only for those copyrighted films for which information is supplied by the producers or distributors.

EB18. Educational Film

The Library of Congress catalogs of film have become, through the years, limited to educational film (see above). Although this guide is focusing on theatrical film, it may be necessary to locate information on educational film. Therefore, a few other sources are listed here. These indexes list films by title, with a brief description, and provide a subject index and directory of distributors.

NICEM (National Information Center for Educational Media). *Index to 16mm Educational Films.* 6th ed. Los Angeles: University of Southern California, 1977. (Began publication in 1967.)

Educational Film Guide. New York: H. W. Wilson, Co., 1936–68(?)

Educational Film Library Association. *Film Evaluation Guide, 1946–1964.* New York: EFLA, 1965. Plus Supplements.

EC. Lists of Films of Individuals (Credits)

The books in this section list films with which an individual was associated. Some are concerned only with performers, such as Dimmitt's *Actor Guide to the Talkies* (no. EC5), Stewart's *Filmarama* (no. EC13), and Weaver's collections of screen credits (nos. EC14 and EC15).

There are filmographies for directors (nos. EC8, EC9, EC10, EC11), for screenwriters (nos. EC2 and EC4), for film editors (no. EC3), for composers (no. EC7), and so on.

The *Screen Achievement Records Bulletin* of the Academy of Motion Picture Arts and Sciences (no. EC1) now gives credits for all crafts involved in making a movie.

Many of the film histories (particularly Section EB) and most biographies (Section G) provide filmographies for individuals.

EC1. Academy of Motion Picture Arts and Sciences. *Screen Achievement Records Bulletin.* Los Angeles: AMPAS, 1934–.

Currently edited by Verna Ramsey. Since 1976 lists films released in Los Angeles, with production data plus full credits: cast, art direction, cinematographers, costume designers, directors, film editors, music, producers, sound, writers. Gives completion date when known. Arranged by film title; international in coverage. Also provides list of individual credits by craft, list of releases by company, index to individual credits. Published three times a year; final volume cumulates the earlier two.

The Screen Achievement Records began with the September 1934 issue of the AMPAS *Bulletin.* It listed work of writers, producers, directors, assistant directors in the production of feature-length films by these studios: Columbia Pictures, Fox Film, MGM Studio, Paramount Studios, RKO Radio Studios, Universal Pictures, Warner Brothers-First National. Also listed photoplays by title and by producing studios.

Format and coverage have varied a great deal. For many years it gave credits for writers and directors only, with a "Reference List of Productions," which named the producer, director, literary source, screenwriter, and adapters. Has also been called the *Bulletin of Screen Achievement Records.* Followed two lists produced by RKO Studios, which included the major Hollywood studios of the time: *Directors and Their Credits, from January 1, 1930 to December 31, 1935* (1935) and *Record of Writers Who Received Screen Credit, during 1932–1934* (1934).

EC2. Academy of Motion Picture Arts and Sciences. *Who Wrote the Movie and What Else Did He Write? An Index of Screen Writers and Their Film Works, 1936–1969.* Leonard Spigelgass, ed. Los Angeles: AMPAS, 1970.

Co-sponsored by AMPAS and Writers Guild of America. West. Lists approximately 2,000 authors, covering 33 years of screen writing. Three separate indexes: writers, titles, and awards. Writers Index lists films with which a writer was associated, as a contributor to script or originator of source material. Film Title Index gives writer's exact association with a particular film (screenplay, screen story, additional dialogue, etc.) as well as original name of literary source (if different). Alternate titles are cross-indexed. Awards Index, limited to writing awards, includes both nominated and award-winning titles; arranged by award and year. Foreign films and writers are included.

American Film Institute. *Catalog.* . . . See no. EB11.

Armes, R. *French Cinema since 1946.* See no. FB11.

EC3. Ash, Rene L. *The Motion Picture Film Editor.* Metuchen, N.J.: Scarecrow Press, 1974.

Lists approximately 650 film editors who have edited moving pictures released in U.S. since the 1920s. Cites their films, including documentaries and television features and specials, along with release date. Section of winners and nominees of awards. Index to film titles.

Birkos, A. S. *Soviet Cinema: Directors and Films.* See no. FB31.

Brosnan, J. *Movie Magic, The Story of Special Effects in the Cinema.* See no. FC24.

Bucher, F. *Germany.* See no. FB15.

EC4. Corliss, Richard, ed. *The Hollywood Screenwriters.* New York: Discus Books/Avon, 1972.

Symposium of interviews and articles on 27 screenwriters, each followed by complete filmography. Concluded by filmographies for 50 writers not discussed in text. Includes silent film writers. Not indexed. Paperback edition. Based on issue of *Film Comment* devoted to Hollywood screenwriter (vol. 6, no. 4, Winter 1970–71) that did index names.

Cowie, P. *Sweden.* See no. FB27.

Cyr, H. W. *A Filmography of the Third World.* See no. EA5.

EC5. Dimmitt, Richard B. *An Actor Guide to the Talkies.* 2 vols. Metuchen, N.J.: Scarecrow Press, 1967–68.

Subtitled: "A Comprehensive Listing of 8,000 Feature-Length Films from January 1949 until December 1964." First volume lists both foreign and domestic films by title, giving cast and date. Cross-references from variant and prior movie titles. Second volume lists about 30,000 performers and refers to films cited in first volume. A supplement, that will cover 1965 through 1974, is planned for late 1977.

Eisenstein, S. *Film Form: Essays in Film Theory and the Film Sense.* See no. FD5.

Film Daily Year Book of Motion Pictures. See no. CA10.

Films in Review. See no. IA8.

Gifford, D. *British Cinema.* See no. FB8.

Huntley, J. *British Film Music.* See no. FC14.

Index de la cinématographie française. See no. EB4.

EC6. Koszarski, Richard, comp. *The Men with the Movie Cameras: 75 Filmographies.* New York: Film Comment, 1972.

Reprints the summer 1972 filmography in *Film Comment* for American cinematographers and adds 15 names. Gives date and director for each film. Index to cameramen.

Lizzani, C. *Storia del cinema italiano.* See no. EB8.

EC7. McCarty, Clifford. *Film Composers in America: A Checklist of Their Work.* Glendale, Calif.: John Valentine, 1953. (Reprinted: DaCapo Press, 1972.)

Lists film composers alphabetically, their films chronologically. Names producing studio. Indexes: film titles, orchestrators.

Manvell, R. *The Film and the Public.* See no. FA10.

Michael, P. *The American Movies Reference Book.* See no. B14.

New York Times Directory of the Film. "Personal Name Index." See no. CB9.

New York Times Film Reviews. See no. H7.

Niver, K. R. *Motion Pictures from the Library of Congress Paper Print Collection.* See no. EA10.

Notable Names in the American Theatre. See no. G8.

EC8. Parish, James R., and Pitts, Michael R. *Film Directors: A Guide to Their American Films.* Metuchen, N.J.: Scarecrow Press, 1974.

Checklist of feature length productions of directors who have made films in U.S. Arranged by director with films listed chronologically. Gives producer (or distributor) and year of release. Includes silent era, serials, and documentaries. Excludes current underground and regional directors. No title index.

EC9. Parish, James R., ed. *Film Directors Guide: Western Europe.* Metuchen, N.J.: Scarecrow Press, 1976.

A companion to his *Film Directors: A Guide to Their American Films,* above. Arranged by director with films listed chronologically in original language, along with American release title when different. Releasing companies are designated for British- and American-made films. Work in U.S. is included if a director established reputation in Europe. Includes early films that are over 40 minutes long. No title index.

All Scandinavia was considered Eastern Europe and therefore excluded from this volume, as was Greece. Future volumes are planned to cover Eastern Europe and Russia, Asia, Africa. A similar volume is planned for release in 1977 for actors of Western Europe.

Perry, G. *The Great British Picture Show.* See no. FB10.

Pudovkin, V. I. *Film Technique and Film Acting.* See no. FD10.

Ragan, D. *Who's Who in Hollywood.* See no. G10.

Rondolino, G. *Dizionario del cinema italiano.* See no. FB23.

Rotha, P. *Documentary Film.* See no. FC5.

Sadoul, G. *Le cinéma français.* See no. FB14.

Sadoul, G. *Histoire du cinéma mondial des origines à nos jours.* See no. FA19.

EC10. Sarris, Andrew. *The American Cinema: Directors and Directions, 1929–1968.* New York: Dutton, 1968.

Discusses 200 directors (according to *auteur* criticism) and lists their films up to 1968. Useful for reference: directorial chronology, which arranges important films by year and director, 1915–67. Directorial index lists every English-language film made after 1929 that is mentioned in book—and in fourteen other sources; gives year and director. No index to directors. Available in paperback (1969).

EC11. *Sight and Sound. Index Series. Special Supplement.* London: British Film Institute, 1943–49.

An old series that is still important. Each number is filmography of works of a single director, compiled by a specialist. Scholarly and reliable. Developed from Jay Leyda's appendix to Sergei M. Eisenstein's *The Film Sense* (see no. FD5), which signaled the need for such compilations.

No. 1. *Erich von Stroheim,* by Herman G. Weinberg (1943)
No. 2. *David Wark Griffith, Part I,* Seymour Stern (1944)
No. 3. *Charles Chaplin,* by Theodore Huff (1945)
No. 4. *D. W. Griffith, Part II(a) "The Birth of a Nation,"* by Seymour Stern (1945)
No. 5. *Fritz Lang,* by Herman G. Weinberg (1946)
No. 6. *Two Pioneers: I, Robert J. Flaherty; II, Hans Richter,* by Herman G. Weinberg (1946)
No. 7. *D. W. Griffith, Part II(b) The Triangle Productions,* by Seymour Stern (1946)
No. 8. *D. W. Griffith, Part II(c) "Intolerance,"* by Seymour Stern (1946)
No. 9. *Ernst Lubitsch,* by Theodore Huff (1947)
No. 10. *D. W. Griffith, Part II(d) "Hearts of the World,"* by Seymour Stern (1947)
No. 11. *Georges Méliès,* by Georges Sadoul (1947)
No. 12. *Alexander Dovzchenko,* by Jay Leyda (1947)
No. 13. *John Ford,* by William Patrick Wootten (1948)
No. 14. *The Cinema and the Negro, 1904–48,* by Peter Noble (1948)
No. 15. *F. W. Murnau,* by Theodore Huff (1948)
No. 16. *Vsevelod I. Pudovkin,* by Jay Leyda (1948)
No. 17. *Josef von Sternberg,* by Curtis Harrington (1949)
No. 18. *Alfred Hitchcock,* by Peter Noble (1949)
Continued by:

EC12. British Film Institute. *New Index Series.* London: British Film Institute, 1950–52.
No. 1. *Carl Dreyer,* by Ebbe Neergaard (1950)

No. 2. *Marcel Carné,* by Jean Queval (1950)
No. 3. *Frank Capra,* by Richard Griffith (1950)
No. 4. *Jean Vigo,* by Joseph and Harry Feldman (1951)
No. 5. *Anthony Asquith,* by Peter Noble (1952)
The series then lapsed, due to lack of funds, until 1958 when indexes for *René Clair,* by Catherine de la Roche, and *Max Ophuls,* by Richard Roud, were published under the National Film Theatre imprint. It was then discontinued.

EC13. Stewart, John, comp. *Filmarama.* Metuchen, N.J.: Scarecrow Press, 1975—.
Vol. 1: *The Formidable Years, 1893–1919* (1975)
Vol. 2: *The Flaming Years, 1920–1929* (1977)
Filmography of Hollywood performers for these periods. Information given (when available): performer's real name and dates, films made during these years. Index to film titles gives year of release (or production date), production or releasing company, and cast (referring to performers in first section). Coverage is quite irregular. Vol. 1 includes Keystone Kops and Mack Sennett Bathing Beauties. Vol. 2 includes "Shakespeare in Silent Films." Series is planned to cover seven decades.

Svensson, A. *Japan.* See no. FB26.

EC14. Weaver, John T., Comp. *Forty Years of Screen Credits 1929–1969.* 2 vols. Metuchen, N.J.: Scarecrow Press, 1970.
Provides screen credits of film stars and also cites their work as director, producer, writer, etc. Arranged by performer with films listed chronologically. Index to names in first volume, with cross-references where necessary. Preceded by:

EC15. Weaver, John T., comp. *Twenty Years of Silents 1908–1929.* Metuchen, N.J.: Scarecrow Press, 1971.
Names performers, directors, and producers of silent films between 1908 and 1928 and lists their known screen credits by year of release. American silent-film studio corporations and distributors also listed. Some talking, part-talking, and synchronized-sound effects releases are included. No title index.

ED. Film Catalogs

Film catalogs list moving pictures that are available for sale or rent and that are primarily intended for programmers of film showings. They can also offer a wealth of information for film research. Many include short films, documentaries, and other films that are not listed in standard filmographies and provide such information as director, stars, release date, country of origin, distributor.

Most of the titles in this section represent the major film catalogs, for example, Artel and Weaver's *Film Programmer's Guide to 16mm Rentals* (no. ED2), Limbacher's *Feature Films on 8mm and 16mm* (no. ED8), and *TV Feature Film Source Book* (no. ED12). Some of the other entries indicate the possibilities of such publications. Consult the following for a more thorough listing of film catalogs:

ED1. Humphrys, Barbara. *Film Programmers' Book List.* Cambridge, Mass.: University Film Study Center, 1973.

ED2. Artel, Linda J., and Weaver, Kathleen, eds. and comps. *Film Programmer's Guide to 16mm Rentals.* San Francisco: San Francisco Community Press, 1972.

Lists over 8,000 films selected from fifty U.S. distributors. Much smaller than Limbacher's *Feature Films* (see no. ED8), and valuable for its selectivity. Reflects popularity of history of film, underground and experimental films, social and political documentaries. Includes short films (which Limbacher does not list); excludes most educational films. Arranged by title with separate listings for documentaries and newsreels. Index to directors.

ED3. *British National Film Catalogue.* London: British Film Institute, 1963–.

Catalogs nonfiction and short films available in Britain for rent, loan, or sale. Includes television programs, both fiction and nonfiction, and other types of 16mm film. Emphasis on British film, but lists films from other countries. Nonfiction films arranged by subject; short fiction films, by title. Each entry gives: distributor, date, technical data, credits, and brief description. Production index includes names, corporations, and government offices. Subject-title index and directory of distributors and production companies. Feature films excluded, because they are described in detail by *Monthly Film Bulletin* (see no. H3). Quarterly; annual cumulation.

ED4. Center for Southern Folklore. *American Folklore Films and Videotapes: An Index.* Memphis, Tenn.: Center for Southern Folklore, 1976.

Lists over 1,800 films and videotapes related to folklore in U.S. Each entry gives length, format, date, producer, distributor, and description. Subject index. List of films by distributors and distributor directory. Annual supplement planned.

ED5. Dawson, Bonnie, comp. *Women's Films in Print: An Annotated Guide to Eight-Hundred 16mm Films by Women.* San Francisco: Booklegger Press, 1975.

Catalog of 800 feature films, shorts, documentaries, available in 16mm for rent or sale, made by 370 American women filmmakers. Arranged by filmmaker, with film arranged alphabetically; each film is briefly described. Directory of distributors. Bibliography: pp. 121–25. Indexes: title and subject. Paperback edition.

ED6. *Film-Makers' Cooperative Catalogue No. 6.* New York: Film-Makers' Cooperative (175 Lexington Ave., N.Y. 10016), 1975.

Catalog of the Cooperative's film-rental library, and, in effect, a guide to American experimental film. Arranged by filmmaker, each film is described by submitter. Index to film titles. Includes international list of distributors of independent films. *Catalogue* is issued irregularly.

ED7. *Films by and/or about Women.* Berkeley, Calif.: Women's History Research Center, 1972.

Subtitle: "Directory of Filmmakers, Films and Distributors, Internationally, Past and Present." Checklist of films available from American distributors. Arranged by topical categories; each film is briefly described. Includes educational and documentary films, films in progress, slide shows, video tapes. Indexes: women filmmakers and their films; distributors and their films. Lacks an index to film themselves.

ED8. Limbacher, James L., comp. and ed. *Feature Films on 8mm and 16mm: A Directory of Feature Films Available for Rental, Sale and Lease in the United States and Canada with Serials and Directors' Indexes.* 5th ed. New York: R. R. Bowker, 1977.

Lists more than 16,000 films available for rent, sale, or lease. Films arranged alphabetically by title with this information: releasing company or country of origin, year of release, running time, special information (color, edition, subtitles, etc.), distributor. Principal cast and director given for feature films. Includes documentaries, experimental film, anthologies, animated film, etc. Separate list of serials. Concludes with directory of film companies and distributors, plus a grouping by area; brief bibliography; index to directors, with their films.

Compiler estimates that he lists approximately 95 percent of films available from major commercial sources. Actually a booker's guide, it lists films available for distribution; earlier editions, therefore, have information not included in this fifth edition. Supplements appear in each issue of *Sightlines* (five times a year), journal of Educational Film Library Association (New York).

ED9. Parlato, Salvatore J., Jr. *Films—Too Good for Words; a Directory of Nonnarrated 16mm Films.* New York: R. R. Bowker, 1972.

Word-free films are grouped by broad categories and briefly described. Information given: distributor, running time, date. Producer/distributor directory. Indexes: titles and subjects.

Parlato has compiled another catalog: *Superfilms: An International Guide to Award Winning Educational Films* (Metuchen, N.J.: Scarecrow Press, 1976).

ED10. Sprecher, Daniel. *Guide to* . . . series. Alexandria, Va.: Serina Press.

Sprecher and the Serina Press have organized many guides for film programmers, providing synopses, index of names, list of sources. Examples:

Guide to Films (16mm) About Famous People. 1969.
Guide to Films (16mm) About Negroes. 1970.
Guide to Free-Loan Films for Entertainment. 1971.
Guide to Free-Loan Sports Films (16mm). 1974.
Guide to Government-Loan Films (16 mm). 1974.
Guide to Free-Loan Films About Foreign Lands (16mm). 1975.

ED11. Task Force on Alternatives in Print. *Alternatives in Print; the Annual Catalog of Social Change Publications.* San Francisco: Glide Publications, 1971– . Annual.

Catalog of books, films, pamphlets, tapes, and records concerned with social change. Arranged by name of distributor or publisher. Consult subject index for "Films"; refers to distributors who rent and sell films about Appalachia, ecology, racisim, war, women, etc.

ED12. *TV Feature Film Source Book.* New York: Broadcast Information Bureau, 1949– . Annual.

Catalog of moving-picture features and other hour-long films either made for or available to television. Part I, Features, gives running time, release date, stars, director, brief description, type or subject of film, any awards, distributor. The 1977 volume lists over 20,000 feature titles. Part II lists sources for films.

EE. Film Scripts

Close study of a film script is often important. Some of the works cited below contain the actual script, for example, the series *Film Scripts* (no. EE2) and Gassner and Nichols's *Twenty Best Film Plays* (no. EE3). Publications that contain filmscripts are indexed by McCarty's *Published Screenplays* (no. EE6), Poteet's *Published Radio, Television and Film Scripts* (no. EE8), and Samples's *Drama Scholars' Index to Plays and Filmscripts* (no. EE9).

Other works in this section tell the reader where a script can be located, e.g., *Primary Cinema Resources* (no. EE11) and Turconi and Bassotto's *Soggetti e sceneggiature* (no. EE10). The catalogs of film book collections (Secton DC) also list film scripts.

L'Avant-scène du cinéma. See no. IA1.

Bianco e nero. See no. IA2.

Bowles, S. E. *An Approach to Film Study.* See no. A1.

British Film Institute. *Catalogue of the Book Library.* "Script Catalog." See no. DC1.

EE1. *Chicorel Theater Index to Plays in Anthologies, Periodicals, Discs and Tapes.* Marietta Chicorel, ed. 3 vols. New York: Chicorel Library Publishing Co., 1970–72.

Indexes screenplays published in anthologies and periodicals in English language. Play titles, playwrights, and anthology editors listed in one alphabet. Separate indexes to authors, plays, editors, and subjects. Subject index lists screenplays separately. Another publication in this series, *Chicorel Index to Film Literature* (New York: 1975, 2 vols.), has no reference value.

EE2. Garrett, George P.; Hardison, O. B.; and Gelfman, Jane R., eds. *Film Scripts.* 4 vols. New York: Appleton-Century-Crofts, 1971–.

Each volume gives final shooting scripts of three classic films, plus appendix, glossary, and bibliography. Bibliography divided into film art and history; screenplays and process of filmmaking; critical works; notes and suggestions for further research; selective list of U.S. film magazines; selected film distributors. Not annotated, but highly recommended.

Film Scripts One contains *Henry V, The Big Sleep, A Streetcar Named Desire*. *Two: High Noon, Twelve Angry Men, The Defiant Ones*. *Three: The Apartment, The Misfits, Charade*. *Four: A Hard Day's Night, The Best Man, Darling*. Editors intend to continue series. All volumes in paperback edition.

EE3. Gassner, John, and Nichols, Dudley, eds. *Twenty Best Film Plays*. New York: Crown, 1943.

Introduction to script writing by Dudley Nichols, a prominent Hollywood screenwriter. Reprints screenplay, not shooting script. Together with annuals listed below, one of few early sources for study of American screenwriting.

Best Film Plays of 1943–1944. Best Film Plays of 1945. John Gassner and Dudley Nichols, eds. (1945, 1946).

Best Moving Pictures of 1922/23; Also Who's Who in the Movies and the Yearbook of the American Screen. Robert E. Sherwood, ed. (1923).

Best Pictures, 1939/40, and the Yearbook of Motion Pictures in America. Jerry Wald and Richard Macaulay, eds. (1940).

Foremost Films of 1938: A Yearbook of the American Film. Frank Vreeland, ed. (1939).

EE4. Ireland, Norma Olin. *Index to Full-Length Plays, 1944–1964*. Boston: F. W. Faxon, 1965.

Indexes plays published in English separately and in collections, 1944–64. Lists authors, titles, and subjects in one alphabet. See Screenplays, Television Plays.

EE5. Laurence, Frank M. "The Shooting Script: Scholarship and Cinema." *American Quarterly* 22, no. 4 (Winter 1970): 912–17.

Names major script collections in U.S. Also discusses the shooting script and difficulties in obtaining them.

EE6. McCarty, Clifford. *Published Screenplays: A Checklist*. Kent, Ohio: Kent State University Press, 1971.

Cites film scripts published in English up to 1970. Locates separately published screenplays as well as those included in writers' handbooks, biographies and autobiographies, monographs on directors, anthologies, periodicals, etc. Intended to be inclusive rather than selective; lists excerpts as well as complete screenplays. Also includes film-novels. Arranged by title; each entry provides: production company and date, director, author and source of screenplay, and full publication information. Name-title index. For screenplays published in foreign languages see Turconi and Bassotto's catalog (no. EE10).

Motion Pictures: A Catalog of Books, Periodicals, Screen Plays and Production Stills. See no. DC3.

New York (City). Public Library. Research Libraries. *Catalog of the Theatre and Drama Collections. Part II: Theatre Collection: Books on the Theatre.* See no. DC4 and DC5.

EE7. *Play Index, 1953–1960.* Estelle A. Fidell, ed. New York: H. W. Wilson, 1963.

———, *1961–1967.* New York: 1968.

———, *1968–1972.* New York: 1973.

Author, title, and subject index to plays, both individual works and those in collections. Film plays listed under Moving Picture Plays. Publisher, date, etc. given with author entry.

EE8. Poteet, G. Howard. *Published Radio, Television and Film Scripts: A Bibliography.* Troy, N.Y.: Whitson Publishing, 1975.

Lists excerpts and complete scripts that have appeared in books and periodicals. Film scripts are listed by title in film section. Limited to English-language sources. Screenwriters and directors are indexed.

Rehrauer, G. *Cinema Booklist* and *Supplements.* See nos. DA9 and DA10.

EE9. Samples, Gordon. *The Drama Scholars' Index to Plays and Filmscripts.* Metuchen, N.J.: Scarecrow Press, 1974.

Subtitled: "A Guide to Plays and Filmscripts in Selected Anthologies, Series and Periodicals." Includes foreign-language sources. For filmscripts, indexes through 1972: *L'Avant-scène du cinéma, Cahiers du cinéma,* and *Cinema* (California); seven American publishers' series; and anthologies that are cited in back of volume. Arrangement, in one alphabet: author of source, screenwriter, director, film title. Complete entry given under screenwriter's name.

Schoolcraft, R. N. *Performing Arts/Books in Print.* See no. DA12.

EE10. Turconi, Davide, and Bassotto, Camillo. *Soggetti e sceneggiature.* Venice: Ed. Mostra Cinema, 1967.

Lists film scripts of 19 countries that can be located in published form or in eleven archives of Europe and U.S. (in U.S.: Academy of Motion Picture Arts and Sciences, Hollywood, and Museum of Modern Art Film Library, New York). Arranged by country, films are listed alphabetically in language of origin. Each entry describes form of the film script. Does not include scripts printed in journals. Index only to countries.

EE11. Wheaton, Christopher D., and Jewell, Richard B., comps. *Primary Cinema Resources: An Index to Screenplays, Interviews and Special Collections at the University of Southern California.* Boston: G. K. Hall, 1975.

Catalogs collections of the Cinema Library, University of Southern California. The first section names studio-produced, mimeographed screenplays in collection. Each entry gives form of the screenplay, year of release, distributor, screenwriter. An index to screenwriters and film personalities follows.

Second section lists interviews and materials on tape. Final section—special collections—includes personal papers, memorabilia, scripts, photographs, etc., but these have been only partially inventoried.

EF. Literary Sources and Film Adaptations

If a student is interested in the background of a moving-picture story, works such as the *Title Guide to the Talkies* (nos. EF1 and EF2), Enser's *Filmed Books and Plays* (no. EF6), and Thiery's *Filmographic Dictionary of World Literature* (no. EF10) will name the original source.

When research requires more information about that source, one could consult the unique Italian *Dizionario letterario Bompiani* (no. EF3), its French counterpart (nos. EF4 and EF5), or the German version (no. EF7). There is nothing quite like this type of work in English, except perhaps the many *Oxford Companions* to literature and theater.

Limbacher's "Remakes, Series and Sequels on Film and Television" (no. EF8) and Thiery (no. EF10) keep track of films that have been made and remade.

Academy of Motion Picture Arts and Sciences. *Screen Achievement Records Bulletin.* See no. EC1.

Academy of Motion Picture Arts and Sciences. *Who Wrote the Movie and What Else Did He Write?* See no. EC2.

American Film Institute. *Catalog* . . . . See no. EB11.

Charensol, G. *Le cinéma.* See no. EA3.

EF1. Dimmitt, Richard B. *A Title Guide to the Talkies.* 2 vols. New York: Scarecrow Press, 1965.

Subtitled: "A Comprehensive Listing of 16,000 Feature Length Films from October 1927 until December 1963." Films are listed alphabetically by title with name of novel, play, poem, short story, or screen story on which movie was based. Gives author's name, publisher, date, or collection in which original work was included. Cross-references from original title to movie title for renamed works. Author index in Vol. 2. English-language sound films only. Use with Dimmitt's *Actor Guide to the Talkies* (see no. EC5) for acting casts. Continued by:

EF2. Aros, Andrew A. *A Title Guide to the Talkies: 1964 through 1974.* Metuchen, N.J.: Scarecrow Press, 1977.

Continues Dimmitt's *Title Guide* . . . , above. Information has been expanded to include foreign films released in U.S. Gives distribution company, year of film's general release, story source, director. (Dimmitt credits producer, but not director.) Authors and screenwriters are indexed, but not directors.

EF3. *Dizionario letterario Bompiani delle opere e dei personaggi di tutti i tempi e di tutte le letterature.* 9 vols. Milan: Bompiani, 1947–50.

———. *Appendice.* 2 vols. Milan: 1964–66.

First seven volumes list and describe works of all periods and countries in literature, art, and music. Consists of articles, arranged alphabetically by Italian form of the work's title, followed by original title in brackets. Index, vol. 9, lists titles in original language with Italian equivalents; also indexes authors. Vol. 8: dictionary of literary *characters,* alphabetized by Italian form of name. Beautifully illustrated. There is a French version of this work:

EF4. *Dictionnaire des oeuvres de tous les temps et de tous les pays: littérature, philosophie, musique, sciences.* Par Laffont-Bompiani. 4th ed. 4 vols. and index. Paris: Société d'Édition de Dictionnaires et Encyclopédies, 1962.

Abridged French edition of Bompiani, above. Lists literary works by French form of title. Author index volume. *Dictionnaire des oeuvres contemporaines de tous les pays* (Paris: 1968) forms a fifth volume.

EF5. *Dictionnaire des personnages littéraires et dramatiques de tous les temps et de tous les pays, Poésie, theatre, roman, musique.* Par Laffont-Bompiani. Paris: Société d'Édition de Dictionnaires et Encyclopédies, 1960.

Companion volume to above. Indentifies and describes characters of fiction, poetry, music, drama. Refers to works cited in volume above.

EF6. Enser, A. G. S. *Filmed Books and Plays.* Revised, cumulated edition. London: A. Deutsch/New York: Academic Press, 1975.

Subtitled: "A List of Books and Plays from Which Films Have Been Made, 1928–1974." Similar to Dimmitt's *Title Guide to the Talkies* (see no. EF1). Gives British version of title, whereas Dimmitt uses American title. Three indexes: film title, author, and change of original title. Film Title Index gives author and publisher of source, original title if different, producer, and date. Author Index arranged by author of source. Change of Original Title Index gives published title of an author's work, followed by screen title when different. Limited to English-language titles.

Film Daily Year Book of Motion Pictures. "Original Titles." See no. CA10.

Halliwell, L. *The Filmgoer's Companion.* See no. A4.

EF7. *Kindlers Literatur Lexikon.* 12 vols. Zurich: Kindler Verlag, 1965–74.

Modeled on Bompiani (no. EF3, above). Entry is by title of literary work, in language of the original. Articles include brief history of the work; summary; and bibliography that lists editions, critical works, adaptations, translations, and also film versions. Includes Eastern as well as Western literature. Twelfth volume provides supplementary section of works, A–Z, and index to entire set: authors, anonymous and collective works, etc.

EF8. Limbacher, James L. "Remakes, Series and Sequels on Film and Television," 3d ed., 1970. In: *A Reference Guide to Film Information* (see no. A5).

Lists material that has been filmed more than once, naming subsequent versions. International coverage. Gives type of source for first production (i.e., book, play, Bible, teleplay, poem, screenplay, etc.), title of first film, along with releasing company or country of origin and year of release—going back to 1900; all known subsequent productions of the same material, with name of releasing company and year of release. Variant titles cross-indexed. Includes list of film series and of films that had sequels.

Two books by Michael B. Druxman can supplement this information: *One Good Film Deserves Another* (South Brunswick and New York: A. S. Barnes and Co., Inc., 1977) discusses film sequels; and *Make It Again, Sam* (A. S. Barnes and Co., Inc., 1975) deals with movie remakes.

McCarty, C. *Published Screenplays: A Checklist.* See no. EE6.

EF9. Sharp, Harold S., and Sharp, Marjorie Z. *Index to Characters in the Performing Arts.* New York: Scarecrow Press.
Part I: *Non-Musical Plays.* 2 vols. 1966
Part II: *Operas and Musical Productions.* 2 vols. 1969.
Part III: *Ballets.* 1972.
Part IV: *Radio and Television.* 1973.

Identifies characters that often appear in moving pictures. Part I: *Non-Musical Plays,* for example, lists characters in plays and identifies their roles. Author and date of play given. Family relationships between characters are generally indicated in one main entry; i.e., the entry for Blanche DuBois refers to Stanley Kowalski (*Streetcar Named Desire*). Major and minor characters included. Limited to plays in English, including those translated into English. Part IV: *Radio and Television* lists both characters and performers in radio and television programs.

EF10. Thiery, Herman. *Dictionnaire filmographique de la litterature mondiale/Filmographic Dictionary of World Literature.* 2 vols. Ghent, Belgium: E. Story-Scientia, 1971–75/Atlantic Highlands, N.J.: Humanities Press, 1971–75.

Sometimes credited to Johan Daisne (pseudonym). Introduced in French, Flemish, English, and German. Main section is arranged by author's name, with this information: title of film, along with original title of source, where this differs; country and year of production; director; performers; any subsequent remakes of film.

A large section of illustrations, mostly studio stills, follows. Index to books and films refers to authors. This index, unfortunately, does not give original title of a film if it is in a language other than those of the dictionary (it generally uses the French version of a title). A supplement is planned.

U.S. Copyright Office. *Motion Pictures. Catalog of Copyright Entries.* . . . See no. EB15.

U.S. Library of Congress. *Library of Congress Catalog.* See no. EB16.

EG. Plot Summaries

A plot summary is sometimes all that is needed. A brief synopsis can be located in many of the annuals (Section CA); the filmographies, both international and national (Sections EA and EB); the film catalogs (Section ED); the film histories (Sections FA and FB); and the genre studies and partial histories (Section FC). See the Subject Index for precise entries.

The books listed below describe selected films, and some rate moving pictures that are shown on television (no. EG4).

EG1. Butler, Ivan. *Cinema in Britain: An Illustrated Survey.* South Brunswick and New York: A. S. Barnes and Co., Inc., 1973.

Briefly describes plot of important British films, giving major technical credits and main cast. Arranged by year of release, 1895 through 1971. Illustrated. Index to films reviewed or mentioned.

EG2. Crowther, Bosley. *The Great Films: Fifty Golden Years of Motion Pictures.* New York: Putnam, 1967.

Crowther, movie critic emeritus of *New York Times,* summarizes and discusses fifty great films from 1915 through 1967. Illustrated. Short bibliography. Paperback edition.

EG3. Garbicz, Adam, and Klinowski, Jacek. *Cinema, the Magic Vehicle: A Guide to its Achievement. Journey One: The Cinema Through 1949.* Metuchen, N.J.: Scarecrow Press, 1975.

Analyzes and describes over 200 films, made from 1913 through 1949, providing screen credits and plot outline. Arranged chronologically. Indexes to directors, film titles.

EG4. Maltin, Leonard, ed. *TV Movies.* New ed. New York: New American Library/Signet Book, 1974.

Evaluates 10,000 films shown on television, plus 300 made-for-TV movies. Provides: director, stars, plot, date, original length, key songs for musicals, capsule summary. Paperback edition.

Two similar books: *Movies on TV,* by Steven H. Scheuer (1978–79 rev. ed., New York: Bantam Books, 1977) and *TV Guide to the Movies* by Judith Crist (New York: Popular Library, 1974).

Scheuer provides director for most entries; Crist does not. Both are paperback editions.

A fuller description is given in the *New York Times Guide to Movies on TV,* edited by Howard Thompson (Chicago: Quadrangle Books, 1970). Limited to films of the 1950s and 1960s, it gives over 2,000 capsule reviews, condensed from the *Times'* film review. Paperback edition.

The *Film Buff's Bible of Motion Pictures,* by D. Richard Baer (see no. EA1), also appraises moving pictures likely to appear on television, but it does not include plot summaries.

Oxford Companion to Film. See no. B16.

EG5. Pickard, R. A. E. *Dictionary of 1,000 Best Films.* New York: Association Press, 1971.

Briefly and critically describes 1,000 films produced in U.S. and abroad since 1903. Production credits and stars are named. Selective, but useful since it credits photography, art direction, music, and editing, which are often difficult to ascertain. Some illustrations. Not indexed.

F. Film Histories

Histories give the main facts and names in the development of moving pictures. Look for those which also provide biographical and bibliographical information. Film histories with detailed indexes can serve to some extent as encyclopedias.

It becomes clear, when reading these books, that they vary with the author. Certain events or theories or contributors might be emphasized or omitted altogether, depending upon the author's individual opinion. Allowances should be made for this situation when gathering material.

FA. International Film Histories

Many general histories have been published, and the following titles are truly a selection. Some are considered standard works, such as Bardeche and Brasillach's *History of Motion Pictures* (no. FA1), Knight's *Liveliest Art* (no. FA7), Ramsaye's *Million and One Nights* (no. FA15), and Rotha's *The Film Till Now* (no. FA18).

Several French works are included (nos. FA6, FA12, FA19, and FA20) because they, too, are important. Even if the reader does not know foreign languages, the bibliographies and filmographies in these books can be useful; a dictionary can help one further.

Others are new and have received both pats and pans from reviewers, but they offer the advantage of recent scholarship; for example, Bohn and Stromgren's *Light and Shadows* (no. FA2), Mast's *Short History of the Movies* (no. FA11), and Rhode's *History of the Cinema* (no. FA16). Several titles are included here because they discuss an important aspect of film, such as Graham's *New Wave* (no. FA4) and O'Leary's *Silent Cinema* (no. FA14).

All of these books either include an index, which makes them handy for reference, or a bibliography, which leads one to other works.

FA1. Bardeche, Maurice, and Brasillach, Robert. *The History of Motion Pictures.* Trans. and edited by Iris Barry. New York: W. W. Norton, 1938. (Reprinted: Arno Press, 1970)
  Classic history of early film, 1895–1936, in Europe and America. Index to film titles and general index. British edition, *History of the Film*, also translated by Iris Barry (1945). Translation of *Histoire du cinéma* (Paris: 1935), which has had many French editions.

FA2. Bohn, Thomas W., and Stromgren, Richard L. *Light and Shadows: A History of Motion Pictures.* Port Washington, N.Y.: Alfred Publishing, 1975.
  High-quality, one-volume history of film that discusses artistic influences as well as industry itself. Selected bibliography, pp. 513–50, arranged by subject. Illustrated with stills. Indexes: name, film title, general. Available in paperback. A second edition is due in 1978.

FA3. Cowie, Peter, ed. *A Concise History of the Cinema.* Screen Series. 2 vols. New York: A. S. Barnes, 1971.
  Vol. 1, before 1940; vol. 2, since 1940. Arranged by country, then by directors with brief outlines of their major films. Generously illustrated. Vol. 1 includes select bibliography. Both volumes index film titles. Paperback edition.

FA4. Graham, Peter, ed. *The New Wave: Critical Landmarks.* Garden City, N.Y.: Doubleday, 1968.
  History of an important movement in contemporary film (French name: *nouvelle vague*). Bibliography, pp. 181–84. Not indexed.

FA5. Jacobs, Lewis. *The Emergence of Film Art.* Cinema Studies Series. New York: Hopkinson and Blake, 1969.
  Subtitled: "The Evolution and Development of the Motion Picture as an Art from 1900 to the Present." Supplements his earlier work, *The Rise of the American Film* (see no FB37); emphasizes aesthetic development of film. Index. Paperback edition.

FA6. Jeanne, Rene, and Ford, Charles, eds. *Histoire encyclopédique du cinéma.* 5 vols. Paris: R. Laffont, 1947–62.
  Scholarly history of world film. Vol. 1: French film, 1895–1929; vol. 2: silent film: Europe (except France), Americas (except U.S.), Africa, Asia, 1895–1923; vol. 3: film of U.S., 1895–1945;

vol. 4: spoken film (except U.S.), 1929–45; vol. 5: postwar film, 1945–55. Bibliography in vol. 5. Indexed.

FA7. Knight, Arthur. *The Liveliest Art: A Panoramic History of the Movies.* New York: Macmillan, 1957.

One of the most important accounts of development of film: 1895 through 1956. Treats film as art, summarizing styles and movements. Excellent annotated list of "One Hundred Best Books on Film," pp. 341–58. List of film sources. Indexes: film titles: general. Available in paperback (New American Library, 1971). A revised edition is due in 1978.

FA8. MacGowan, Kenneth. *Behind the Screen: The History and Techniques of the Motion Picture.* New York: Delacorte Press, 1965.

Records technical development of film, from inventions of early 19th century into 1960s. Scholarship in this area is difficult since few records were kept in the early days; primary sources are mostly patents and catalogs. Instructive illustrations. Index. Available in paperback (Dell Publishing Co., 1967).

FA9. Manvell, Roger. *Film.* Rev. and enl. ed. Harmondsworth, Eng.: Penguin Books, 1950.

Brief historical survey; important for its analysis of the art and social aspects of film. Critically annotated book list, pp. 251–63. Index to film titles, names, and subjects.

FA10. Manvell, Roger. *The Film and the Public.* Harmondsworth, Eng.: Penguin Books, 1955.

Useful for supplements: (1) Annotated bibliography of film history, art of film, screenplays and books about individual films, film and society, television. (2) Studies of individual film directors, with books and articles in English by and about directors. (3) List of selected films and filmmakers, arranged by time period, then director.

FA11. Mast, Gerald. *A Short History of the Movies.* 2d ed. Indianapolis: Bobbs-Merrill Co., 1975.

Completely revised and expanded version of 1971 publication (and not so short anymore). "Appendix for Further Reading and Viewing" matches important books and films with chapters. Illustrated with film stills. Index to names, film titles, subjects. Paperback edition.

FA12. Mitry, Jean. *Histoire du cinéma, art et industrie.* 3 vols. Paris: Éd. Universitaires, 1967–73.

An important history of film; discusses both art and industry. Vol. 1 covers 1895 through 1914; vol. 2, 1915–25; vol. 3, 1923–30. Table of contents at back. List of works cited; illustrated. Four indexes in vol. 3 for set: names of directors, performers, etc.; titles of French films and of French version of foreign films; original titles of foreign films; corporate names.

FA13. Niver, Kemp R. *The First Twenty Years: A Segment of Film History*. Los Angeles: Locare Research Group, 1968.

Mostly a pictorial history, covering 1894 through 1913, with some description of over 100 films from Library of Congress copyright collection. Indexes films by title and by date, giving producer and copyright date. Index to names cited. Can serve as adjunct to his *Motion Pictures from the Library of Congress Paper Print Collection* (see no. EA10).

FA14. O'Leary, Liam. *The Silent Cinema*. London: Studio Vista, 1965.

Discusses 140 pictures made during silent era. International, with emphasis on American film. Well illustrated. Index to performers, directors, and producers. Available in paperback (Dutton).

FA15. Ramsaye, Terry. *A Million and One Nights: A History of the Motion Pictures*. 2 vols. New York: Simon and Schuster, 1964.

Concerned with silent era; the first history to treat film as serious art. Although an inside story rather than a scholarly study, it remains an important source of information. First published in 1926. No list of sources. Index in vol. 2. Paperback edition.

FA16. Rhode, Eric. *A History of the Cinema: From its Origins to 1970*. New York: Hill & Wang, 1976.

Chronological discussion of film history, relating movies to their social and economic context. Bibliography, pp. 641–49, coordinates readings with chapters. Illustrated; indexed. Available in paperback (1977).

FA17. Robinson, David. *The History of World Cinema*. New York: Stein and Day, 1973.

A general history. Provides selected filmographies for directors mentioned in text, pp. 356–417. Illustrated. Indexes: general, film titles, names. Available in paperback (1974). Published in England as: *World Cinema, A Short History* (London: Eyre Methuen, 1973).

FA18. Rotha, Paul. *The Film Till Now. A Survey of World Cinema.* New edition by Richard Griffith. Feltham, Eng.: Hamlyn House, 1967.
   A standard work first published in 1930; it has had numerous editions. Parts 1 and 2, "The Film Till Now," comprise the original text by Rotha, which talks about film up to 1929. Richard Griffith added Part 3, "The Film Since Then," in 1949. It discusses American and European film from 1929 to 1948 and provides glossaries of technical and general terms. In 1960 Griffith added an "Epilogue" that surveys filmmaking countries of the world from 1948 through 1958. The 1967 edition adds a "Postscript," written by Rotha, that briefly summarizes developments in world cinema during early 1960s. Everything tied together by detailed index.

FA19. Sadoul, Georges. *Histoire du cinéma mondial des origines à nos jours.* 9. éd., revue et augmentée. Paris: Flammarion, 1972.
   One-volume panorama of cinema covering 85 countries, written by one of France's foremost film historians. Especially useful since it discusses countries not generally included in histories. Includes: filmographies of 200 directors; chronology of 5,000 films of fifty countries, 1892–1972; list of principal works consulted, arranged by country and evaluated by author. Table of contents at back. Illustrated. Indexes: films, names, terms, national cinemas.

FA20. Sadoul, Georges. *Histoire générale du cinéma.* 6 vols. Édition revue et augmentée. Avec la collaboration de Bernard Eisenschitz. Paris: Denoël, 1973–75.
   Standard history in six parts. Vol. 1 covers 1832–97, the beginnings (3d ed.); vol. 2, 1897–1909, the pioneers (3d ed.); vols. 3 and 4, 1909–20, before and during the war years (2d ed.); vols. 5 and 6, 1919–29, silent film in Europe and in Hollywood. Each volume has chronology of principal films of period and index to names and films cited. Tables of contents in back.
   Future volumes planned. The original edition (5 vols., Paris: Denoël, 1946–54) includes a volume that covers 1939–54.

Turconi, D., and Bassotto, C. *Il film e la sua storia.* See no. DA13.

FB. National Film Histories

These histories are concerned with the moving pictures of

individual countries. They all have more to offer than facts alone: a bibliography that refers one to other works; a filmography of that country's moving pictures; or some other reference feature. Countries included:

Africa	India
China	Italy
Eastern Europe	Japan
England	Scandinavia
France	Soviet Union
Germany	United States

Africa

FB1. *Les cinémas africains en 1972.* Par Guy Hennebelle. *L'Afrique Littéraire et Artistique 20.* Paris: Société africaine d'édition, 1972.

Surveys contemporary African cinema, principally in Egypt, Algeria, Tunisia, Morocco, Mauritainia, Senegal, Ivory Coast, Nigeria, Guinea, Gabon, Congo. National filmographies supplied for most countries as well as individual filmographies for several directors. Dictionary of 168 African filmmakers; excellent bibliography, pp. 347–66. Table of contents in back.

China

FB2. Leyda, Jay. *Dianying: An Account of Films and the Film Audience in China.* Cambridge: Massachusetts Institute of Technology Press, 1972.

Presents history of Chinese film from 1896 through 1967. Based on films studied in Peking's Film Archives. Appendices include: biographical dictionary of contributors to the art and history of Chinese films; list of important films made by Chinese and foreign groups from 1897 to 1966; list of sources. Well illustrated; index.

Eastern Europe

FB3. Hibbin, Nina. *Eastern Europe: An Illustrated Guide.* Screen Series. South Brunswick and New York: A.S. Barnes and Co., Inc., 1969.

Guide to post-World War II work of film directors, performers, and technicians in Albania, Bulgaria, Czechoslovakia, East Germany, Hungary, Poland, Romania, the Soviet Union, and Yugoslavia. Individuals are listed only by their homeland, so one must know their nationality. Index to films cited, but not to names. Available in paperback.

FB4. Liehm, Mira, and Liehm, Antonin J. *The Most Important Art: Eastern European Film After 1945.* Berkeley: University of California Press, 1977.
Describes postwar film of Eastern European countries. Selected bibliography includes important books and periodicals published in English and foreign languages. Illustrated. Indexes to films and names.

Antonin Liehm is also author of *Closely Watched Films: The Czechoslovak Experience* (White Plains, N.Y.: International Arts and Sciences Press, 1974). Interviews with 32 Czech and Slovak filmmakers and selected filmography, arranged by director. Indexes to names and films.

FB5. Nemeskúrty, István. *Word and Image: History of the Hungarian Cinema.* 2d ed. New York: International Publications Service, 1974.
Surveys Hungarian film from 1896 through early 1970s. Most useful for its record of feature films made between 1945 and 1974, which names directors and leading performers. Illustrated. Index to films mentioned in text. First published in 1968.

FB6. Stoil, Michael John. *Cinema Beyond the Danube: The Camera and Politics.* Metuchen, N.J.: Scarecrow Press, 1974.
Brief introduction to moving pictures of Eastern Europe, from beginnings to present. Covers Bulgaria, Czechoslovakia, Hungary, Poland, Soviet Union. Bibliography of works available in English. Illustrated. Index of films (gives country of origin, production year, director); general index.

England

Butler, I. *Cinema in Britain.* See no. EG1.

FB7. Durgnat, Raymond. *A Mirror for England: British Movies from Austerity to Affluence.* New York: Praeger, 1971.
Chatty survey of major themes in British films, from 1945 through late sixties. Recommended for its reference addenda: (1) bibliography, pp. 270–82, which cites books and articles on British directors and films; (2) filmographic index, pp. 283–322,

which lists films of this period by title, giving date and principals; (3) indexes to British film artists, foreign film artists and their films, and other names.

FB8. Gifford, Denis. *British Cinema: An Illustrated Guide.* International Film Guide Series. South Brunswick and New York: A.S. Barnes and Co., Inc., 1968.

Lists people involved in British film since its beginning. Index to all films cited, totaling 5,000 titles. Illustrated. Paperback edition.

FB9. Low, Rachael, and Manvell, Roger. *The History of the British Film 1896-1906.* London: Allen & Unwin, 1948.

Low, Rachael. *The History of the British Film 1906-1929.* 3 vols. London: Allen & Unwin, 1949—71.

Sponsored by British Film Institute. Basic, scholarly history of early British film, 1896 through 1929. Concerned primarily with the industry, although it also discusses individual films. Each volume lists primary sources for research. Illustrated; indexes names and film titles.

FB10. Perry, George. *The Great British Picture Show; from the 90s to the 70s.* New York: Hill & Wang, 1974.

Surveys 75 years of British film. "Biographical Guide to the British Cinema," pp. 285–339, provides brief biography and filmography of major British film people. Bibliography. Illustrated; index.

France

FB11. Armes, Roy. *French Cinema since 1946.* 2d enlarged edition. International Film Guide Series. 2 vols. South Brunswick and New York: A.S. Barnes and Co., Inc., 1970.

History of French film, covering 1946 to 1970, arranged by director. Concludes with filmography and select bibliography for each. Index to film titles. Paperback edition.

FB12. Jeanne, René, and Ford, Charles. *Histoire encyclopédique de cinéma.* Tome 1: *Le cinéma français, 1895–1929.* 7. éd. Paris: Robert Laffont, 1947.

Well-documented history of early French film. Illustrated; index. (Also see no. FA6.)

FB13. Martin, Marcel. *France: An Illustrated Guide to 400 Key*

Figures in the French Cinema. Screen Series. South Brunswick and New York: A.S. Barnes and Co., Inc., 1971.
Brief biographical information on performers and directors, past and present. Strives to include underrated personalities and promising newcomers. Paperback edition.

FB14. Sadoul, Georges. *Le cinéma français, 1890–1962.* Paris: Flammarion, 1962.
Compact history of French film beginning with Lumière and Méliès, ending with *nouvelle vague* in 1961. Also lists works of 200 French directors and chronology of French films, 1892–1960. No bibliography. Illustrated. Indexes films and names. Table of contents at back. Also published in France as *Histoire du cinéma français.* English version, *French Film* (London: Falcon Press, 1953), provides only the history and ends with 1950. Illustrated; indexed.

Germany

FB15. Bucher, Felix. *Germany.* Screen Series. South Brunswick and New York: A.S. Barnes and Co., Inc., 1970.
Dictionary of people associated with film in Germany. Provides brief biography and list of films. Emphasis on German film before 1945, especially between 1919 and 1933. Index to films cited. Paperback edition.

FB16. Eisner, Lotte H. *The Haunted Screen, Expressionism in the German Cinema and the Influence of Max Reinhardt.* Berkeley: University of California Press, 1969.
History of an important period in German film, 1913–33. Bibliography of works cited; selective filmography, with casts. Illustrations; index. Paperback edition.

FB17. Kracauer, Siegfried. *From Caligari to Hitler: A Psychological History of the German Film.* Princeton, N.J.: Princeton University Press, 1947.
A basic study in film history and propaganda. Analyzes German film, and more specifically, German "screen motifs" from 1895 to 1933. Bibliography; index. Available in paperback.

FB18. Manvell, Roger, and Fraenkel, Heinrich. *The German Cinema.* New York: Praeger, 1971.
History of German cinema from 1895 through the 1960s. Bibliography. Indexes: principal names and films.

India

FB19. Barnouw, Erik, and Krishnaswamy, S. *Indian Film.* New York: Columbia University Press, 1963.

History of Indian film industry from beginnings through 1962. Bibliography, mostly of English-language sources. Index.

Can be updated with *Seventy-five Years of Indian Cinema* by Firoze Rangoonwalla (New Delhi: Indian Book Co., 1975). Covers Indian film from 1896 to 1975. Index to film titles.

Italy

Annuario del cinema italiano. See no. CA3.

FB20. Jarratt, Vernon. *Italian Cinema.* National Cinema Series. London: Falcon Press, 1951. (Reprinted: Arno Press, 1972)

Surveys film in Italy up to 1950 with emphasis on 1930s and 1940s. Appendices: list of films, 1928–48, by leading Italian directors; cast and credit lists for some important postwar films. Illustrated. Indexes: film titles and names. Continued by Rondi's *Italian Cinema Today* (see no. FB22).

FB21. Leprohon, Pierre. *The Italian Cinema.* New York: Praeger, 1972.

Surveys history of Italian film from 1895 through 1969. Includes biographical dictionary of 150 important film people and bibliography. Illustrated. Names and films indexed. Available in paperback (1973). This translation revises and expands the original French text, *Le cinéma italien; histoire, chronologie, biographies, filmographies, documents, imagiens* (Paris: Seghers, 1966). The French edition does, however, provide a detailed chronology of Italian film, production and economic statistics, and filmography with credits, in addition to biographies and bibliography.

Lizzani, C. *Storia del cinema italiano.* See no. EB8.

FB22. Rondi, Gian Luigi. *Italian Cinema Today, 1952–1965.* Foreword by Bosley Crowther. N.Y.: Hill & Wang, 1966.

Illustrated account of Italian films from 1952 through 1965. Supplements Jarratt's *Italian Cinema* (no. FB20, above). Indexes: performers and directors, film titles, producers.

FB23. Rondolino, Gianni. *Dizionario del cinema italiano 1945–1969.* Turin: G. Einaudi, 1969.

Brief biographies of people involved in film of postwar, Italy. Includes directors, screenwriters, scenarists, performers, cameramen, designers, musicians, producers; filmography for each person. "Nota bibliografica" lists major general works and monographs on Italian film. Continues biographical section in Pasinetti's *Filmlexikon* (see no. B17).

Japan

FB24. Anderson, Joseph L., and Richie, Donald. *The Japanese Film: Art and Industry.* New York: Grove Press, 1960.

Discusses Japanese film from 1896 through 1959, and analyzes its content and technique. Illustrated. Film titles in index given both in Japanese and English. Indexed. Paperback edition.

FB25. Richie, Donald. *Japanese Cinema, Film Style and National Character.* Garden City, N.Y.: Doubleday & Co., 1971.

Covers history of Japanese film from the beginnings through 1970. Lists films available from distributors in 16mm. Illustrated with stills. Names and English and Japanese versions of film titles are indexed. Revises and expands his 1961 *Japanese Movies.*

FB26. Svensson, Arne. *Japan.* Screen Series. South Brunswick and New York: A. S. Barnes and Co., Inc., 1971.

Small encyclopedia of film people and important films, arranged in one alphabet. For people: brief biography and filmography; for films, arranged by Japanese title: English-language release titles, credits and cast, summary plot, comment by Svensson. Glossary of terms. Illustrated. Index to 2,000 film titles gives both Japanese and English (or American) versions. Paperback edition.

Scandinavia

FB27. Cowie, Peter. *Sweden.* In collaboration with Arne Svensson. Screen Series. 2 vols. South Brunswick and New York: A. S. Barnes and Co., Inc., 1970.

Sweden 1: dictionary of directors, performers, writers, technicians, etc., with credits; and of plot outlines of important films. Index to film titles in Swedish and English. Companion volume, Sweden 2, assesses themes, trends, directors, and provides a bibliography.

Supplement with Stig Björkman's *Film in Sweden: The New*

Directors (South Brunswick and New York: A. S. Barnes and Co., Inc., 1977), which spotlights ten directors who have made films in Sweden since 1963. Provides filmographies for each.

FB28. Hardy, Forsyth. *Scandinavian Film.* National Cinema Series. London: Falcon Press, 1952. (Reprinted: Arno Press, 1972.)

This classic work summarizes Danish, Swedish, and Norwegian film through 1940s, with emphasis on Sweden. Illustrated. Index to film titles and names.

FB29. Hillier, Jim, ed. *Cinema in Finland: An Introduction.* London: British Film Institute, 1975/New York: Zoetrope, 1977.

Brief introduction to history, traditions, important figures of this national cinema. Describes most films that the Finnish Film Archive can provide for noncommercial screenings abroad. Pamphlet format.

Finnish Cinema, by Peter Cowie (South Brunswick and New York: A. S. Barnes and Co., Inc., 1976), surveys the film of Finland, with special attention to New Wave period. Section of major names, with filmographies. Bibliography. Index to film titles.

Soviet Union

FB30. Babitsky, Paul, and Rimberg, John. *The Soviet Film Industry.* New York: Praeger, 1955.

History of Russian film, 1917–53. Describes Soviet takeover of the industry and its subsequent control. Appendix III provides biographical information on some directors. No bibliography, but each chapter concludes with full notes. Separate indexes to films, persons, subjects. Film index gives date, scenarist, and director.

A bibliography of works dealing with Soviet film is available in the *Soviet Cinema, Film and Photography. A Selected Annotated Bibliography,* compiled by Louis Harris Cohen (Edwards Air Force Base, Calif.: Air Force Flight Test Center, 1975). For materials in English see section: "The Soviet Cinema in Foreign Languages: A Selected List." Also includes a glossary of abbreviations and acronyms and a dictionary of cinematographic terms. Index to names. Prepared for his doctoral dissertation: *The Cultural-Political Traditions and Developments of the Soviet Cinema 1917–1972* (New York: Arno Press, 1974).

FB31. Birkos, Alexander S., comp. *Soviet Cinema: Directors and Films.* Hamden, Conn.: Archon Books, 1976.

Guide to careers and films of Russian filmmakers from 1918 to 1975. Arranged in two sections; first: lists directors, with brief biography, films, and any publications available in English (including important periodical articles). Second section: selected list of Soviet films released during these years, providing director, story source, brief description, critical reception. Soviet film studios are listed by city. General, selected bibliography. Illustrated.

FB32. Leyda, Jay. *Kino: A History of the Russian and Soviet Film.* Atlantic Highlands, N.J.: Humanities Press, 1960.

Scholarly history of Russian film from 1896 through 1947; brief postscript summarizes 1948 through 1958. Appendices include: first documentary series filmed in Russia; select list of films from 1908 through 1958, including directors and casts; research sources. Illustrated; index. Available in paperback (Macmillan, 1973).

United States

FB33. Brownlow, Kevin. *The Parade's Gone By.* New York: Alfred A. Knopf, 1968.

Tells story of silent film through interviews with the greats of that era. Tied together with Brownlow's commentary. Illustrated; index. Available in paperback (University of California Press, 1976).

FB34. Griffith, Richard, and Mayer, Arthur. *The Movies.* Rev. ed., with the assistance of Eileen Bowser. New York: Simon and Schuster, 1970.

History of American moving pictures; primarily pictorial, brief text. Arranged chronologically, beginning with kinetoscope and ending with films of 1969. Names and film titles indexed. Good example of the pictorial guide. Available in paperback (1975).

FB35. Hampton, Benjamin B. *History of the American Film Industry, from its Beginnings to 1931.* New York: Dover Publications, 1970.

Introduction by Richard Griffith. Important history of American film industry through 1930. Good summary of the patent wars. Reprints, without change, *A History of the Movies* (New York: 1931). Index. Paperback edition.

FB36. Hendricks, Gordon. *Origins of the American Film.* New York: Arno Press, 1972.
Gathers three earlier works by Hendricks, with a new introduction: *The Edison Motion Picture Myth* (1961); *Beginning of the Biograph* (1964); *The Kinetoscope: America's First Commercially Successful Motion Picture Exhibitor* (1966). Intended to balance Ramsaye's *A Million and One Nights* (see no. FA15), this history acknowledges the contributions of W. K. L. Dickson. A chronology serves as outline. Index.

FB37. Jacobs, Lewis. *The Rise of the American Film: A Critical History.* New York: Teachers College Press, Columbia University, 1968.
Subtitled: "With an Essay, Experimental Cinema in America, 1921–1947." An important and detailed history of American film from 1896 through 1939. Supplement surveys experimental cinema from 1921 to 1947. Bibliography, pp. 583–606, lists books, documents, catalogs and press sheets, periodicals, etc., by time periods, resulting in a chronology of film literature up to 1939. Indexes: film titles, names, general. Paperback edition. (First edition, published in 1939, lacked essay on experimental cinema.)

FB38. Jobes, Gertrude. *Motion Picture Empire.* Hamden, Conn.: Archon Books, 1966.
Well-researched history of the movie business. Bibliography, pp. 373–81, gives useful list of newspapers and periodicals. Index.

FC. Genre Studies & Partial Histories

Those films which fall into distinctive types of style or purpose are called genre films. Examples are science fiction, mysteries, Westerns. This section includes books that concentrate on genre studies as well as works that deal with a particular aspect of moving pictures, such as music, blacks, women.
Categories included:
    Blacks in Moving Pictures
    Documentary Films
    Fantasy in Moving Pictures
    Music and Musicals

Mystery, Crime, Spy Films
Serials
Underground Film
Westerns
Women in Moving Pictures

Blacks in Moving Pictures

FC1. Mapp, Edward. *Blacks in American Films: Today and Yesterday.* Metuchen, N.J.: Scarecrow Press, 1972.
   Analyzes blacks as major characters in films, from silents through 1970. Only American-made movies and Afro-American roles are considered (African characters excluded). Bibliography. pp. 255–67. Index to names and film titles.
   Can be used with another study of black stereotypes: *Toms, Coons, Mulattoes, Mammies and Bucks: An Interpretive History of Blacks in American Films,* by Donald Bogle (New York: Viking Press, 1973), a chronological account. Illustrated; names and film titles indexed.

FC2. Noble, Peter. *The Negro in Films.* London: S. Robinson, 1948. (Reprinted: Arno Press, 1970)
   Examines role of blacks in American films from 1902 through World War II and contrasts this with blacks as depicted in European films. Early chapters are important, but rest of text is quite dated. Still useful for appendices: bibliography of books on general aspects of race relations in U.S.; list of articles, books, and sections in books about blacks in film; list of films covering 1902–48 that feature blacks or contain important racial themes, grouped by American, British, and Continental. Illustrated; index. Supplement with a book due to be published in late 1977: *Blacks in Black and White: A Source Book on Black Films,* by Henry T. Sampson (Metuchen, N.J.: Scarecrow Press).

Powers, A. *Blacks in American Movies.* See no. DA8.

Documentary Films

Baddeley, W. H. *The Technique of Documentary Film Production.* See no. FD12.

FC3. Barnouw, Erik. *Documentary: A History of the Non-Fiction Film.* New York: Oxford University Press, 1974.
   Traces documentary film from work of the Lumière brothers

through films from Vietnam War. International in scope: the author viewed 700 nonfiction films in 20 countries (all major film centers except China and Cuba). Bibliography, pp. 297–311. Illustrated; index. Available in paperback.

FC4. Fielding, Raymond. *The American Newsreel, 1911–1967.* Norman: University of Oklahoma Press, 1972.

History of one type of documentary. Bibliography, pp. 351–75, includes books, articles, dissertations. Illustrated; index.

FC5. Rotha, Paul. *Documentary Film.* 3d ed., rev. and enl., in collaboration with Sinclair Road and Richard Griffith. New York: Hastings House, 1963. (Reprinted: London: Secker and Warburg, 1973.)

Subtitled: "The Use of the Film Medium to Interpret Creatively and in Social Terms the Life of the People as It Exists in Reality." A standard history of documentary film, originally published in 1936. Summarizes national developments by country. Credits given for 100 important documentary films. Brief bibliography. Indexes: films, names, general topics. 1936 edition (London) has appendix listing major documentary directors and their principal films.

Fantasy in Moving Pictures

FC6. Edera, Bruno. *Full Length Animated Feature Films.* Visual Communication Books. New York: Hastings House, 1977.

History and catalog of full-length animated films. International in coverage. Catalog is arranged by country, each film listed chronologically; followed by index to films, which is also arranged by country of origin. Bibliography includes articles, catalogs, reviews. Illustrated. General index to names, but not to film titles.

FC7. Halas, John and Manvell, Roger. *The Technique of Film Animation.* 4th ed. Library of Communication Techniques. London/New York: Hastings House, 1976.

Thorough discussion of film animation, including television commercials, educational and experimental film, and cartoons. Appendix includes glossary of terms, selected book list. Profusely illustrated; index.

FC8. Lee, Walt. *Reference Guide to Fantastic Films: Science Fiction, Fantasy and Horror.* 3 vols. Los Angeles: Chelsea-Lee Books, 1972–74.

Films of fantasy are arranged alphabetically by original title with this information (when available): English version of title, title variants, nationality, date, studio/distributors, credits, film description, type, citations to published literature. "Fantastic" includes any exception to reality: science fiction, horror, mystery, mythology, satire, surrealism, animated features, the supernatural, dream sequences, and musicals if fantasy is significant. Films from Asia, Africa, Europe included when information was available. Bibliography, end of Vol. 3. Illustrated. Paperback edition.

FC9. Parish, James R., and Pitts, Michael R. *The Great Science Fiction Pictures.* Metuchen, N.J.: Scarecrow Press, 1977.

Filmography of important science fiction pictures with credits and synopsis; includes foreign films released in U.S. Also lists science fiction shows on radio and television. Selected bibliography; illustrated; not indexed.

FC10. Rovin, Jeff. *The Fabulous Fantasy Films.* South Brunswick and New York: A.S. Barnes and Co., Inc., 1977.

Deals with moving pictures "in which the situations are far removed from the realm of reason or possibility." Appendix provides cast and credits of 500 fantasy films. Index to names and film titles.

Music and Musicals

FC11. Burton, Jack. *The Blue Book of Hollywood Musicals.* Watkins Glen, N.Y.: Century House, 1953.

Subtitled: "Songs from the Sound Tracks and the Stars Who Sang Them Since the Birth of the Talkies a Quarter-Century Ago." Anthology of Hollywood musicals covering twenty-five years from 1927, when the first talkie was made, to October 31, 1952. Films arranged by year and also by four groups: musicals (song and dance productions), feature films with songs, Western films with songs, and full-length cartoon films with songs. Each entry gives director, stars, and songs in that production. Lists albums of Hollywood musicals and singing and dancing stars with film in which they made their debut. Illustrated. Index to film titles. Woll's *Songs from Hollywood Musical Comedies* (see no. FC18) gives similar information, bringing Burton up to date. Songs can be located with the index below:

FC12. Burton, Jack. *The Index of American Popular Music.* Watkins Glen, N.Y.: Century House, 1957.

Indexes songs in *Blue Book of Hollywood Musicals,* above, as well as Burton's other musical Blue Books (for Broadway and Tin Pan Alley). Arranged by song title.

FC13. Hippenmeyer, Jean-Roland. *Jazz sur Films, ou 55 années de rapports jazz-cinéma vus à travers plus de 800 films tournés entre 1917 et 1972.* Yverdon, Switzerland: Éditions de la Thièle, 1973.

Filmography of films made between 1917 and 1972 that feature jazz music or musicians. Includes short films and documentaries as well as feature length. Arranged by year. International in coverage, although majority of titles are American. Also includes list of films with jazz background music. Indexes to film titles, and to musicians, performers, and directors.

There is another compilation, by David Meeker: *Jazz in the Movies: A Guide to Jazz Musicians, 1917-1977* (London: Talisman Books, 1977. Distributed in U.S. by Arlington House).

FC14. Huntley, John. *British Film Music.* London: Skelton Robinson, 1947. (Reprinted: Arno Press, 1972).

History of music in British film through mid-1940s. Biographical index is a who's who of film music composers, music directors, sound recordists, sound track stars and film music writers; gives brief background and film credits. Lists recordings of British film music. Bibliography.

FC15. Limbacher, James L., comp. and ed. *Film Music: From Violins to Video.* Metuchen, N.J.: Scarecrow Press, 1974.

This volume matches composers with their films, after a discussion of the early days and a collection of essays by various composers. Chapters 9 through 12: list films by title, giving release date; arrange films by year of release, naming composers or musical directors; list composers and films credited to them; list recorded musical scores. International in scope; covers 1908 through 1972.

McCarty, C. *Film Composers in America.* See no. EC7.

FC16. Manvell, Roger, and Huntley, John. *The Technique of Film Music.* Revised edition by Richard Arnell and Peter Day. Library of Communication Techniques. New York: Hastings House, 1975.

Appendices provide outline history of film music; selected list of film music recordings; selected bibliography of books, articles and parts of books arranged chronologically by publication date. Illustrated; index. Originally published in 1957.

Salem, J. M. *A Guide to Critical Reviews. Part II: The Musical.* See no. H8.

FC17. Taylor, John Russell, and Jackson, Arthur. *The Hollywood Musical.* New York: McGraw-Hill, 1971.

First part discusses the musical. Second part: selected filmography of approximately 275 best-known musicals giving full credits as well as songs. Separate indexes list more than 1,100 individuals who have contributed to musicals; about 2,750 song titles, cross-referenced to the filmography; and 1,443 musical titles. Illustrated.

FC18. Woll, Allen L. *Songs from Hollywood Musical Comedies, 1927 to the Present: A Dictionary.* New York: Garland Publishing, 1976.

Provides access to songs from Hollywood musicals. First section names over 7,000 songs and the Hollywood musical each came from. Second section lists films by title with this information: date, stars, director, composer and lyricist (if work is attributable), available soundtrack recordings of score. Songs are named for musicals that have been recorded and for musicals produced *after* 1950, because this information is not available elsewhere. (See Jack Burton's *Blue Book of Hollywood Musicals*, no. FC11, for musicals prior to 1950.) The 1,187 musical comedies indexed are also grouped by date. Index to composers and lyricists.

Mystery, Crime, Spy Films

FC19. Parish, James R., and Pitts, Michael R. *The Great Gangster Pictures.* Edited by T. Allan Taylor. Metuchen, N.J.; Scarecrow Press, 1976.

Filmography, with full credits and synopsis, of major gangster pictures; excludes detective films. Limited mostly to U.S.-produced features, with a few European films. Introductory essay. Illustrated; not indexed.

FC20. Parish, James R., and Pitts, Michael R. *The Great Spy Pictures.* Edited by T. Allan Taylor. Metuchen, N.J.: Scarecrow Press, 1974.

Filmography of major spy pictures with full credits and synopsis; includes European films released in U.S. Introductory essay. Selected bibliography of spy novels and series. Illustrated; not indexed. First in series of reference sources for film genre.

FC21. Steinbrunner, Chris, and Penzler, Otto. *Encyclopedia of Mystery and Detection.* New York: McGraw-Hill, 1976.

Entries for mystery writers, major fictional detectives, sidekicks, and adversaries include plot synopses of key works, critical appraisal, checklists of complete works, and any moving pictures, plays, radio and television series based on these works. An example: following biography of Agatha Christie is a checklist of her mysteries not about Miss Marple or Poirot (they have their own entries), then films of her works. Moving picture listings give release date, main cast, director, writer, producing company, plot summary. Spy, crime, adventure stories, gothic romances are all included. Illustrated, including moving picture stills. No entries or cross-references for film titles; no index.

Serials

FC22. Lahue, Kalton C. *Continued Next Week: A History of the Moving Picture Serial.* Norman: University of Oklahoma Press, 1964. (Reprinted: 1969.)

History of silent film serials in U.S. Appendix lists serials from 1912 to 1930 with directors (when known), cast, release date, studio, and chapter titles. Indexes: names, titles, general. Supplements chronology of serials of the sound era in Weiss and Goodgold's *To Be Continued . . .,* below.

FC23. Weiss, Ken, and Goodgold, Ed. *To Be Continued. . . .* New York: Crown, 1972.

Chronology of serials of the sound era, 1929 through 1956. Serials arranged by year, giving studio, number of episodes, cast, and plot outline. Summary list of serials in back, arranged alphabetically by year. Illustrated. Index to all names and serial titles. Supplements silent film serials in Lahue's *Continued Next Week,* above.

Special Effects

FC24. Brosnan, John. *Movie Magic, The Story of Special Effects in the Cinema.* New York: St. Martin's Press, 1974.

Special effects in moviemaking from early days. Appendix includes "Notes on Some Movie Magicians," which lists 40 special effects men, mostly American, with their well-known films. List of Academy Award winners for special effects. Indexes to personal names, film titles, and subjects and techniques.

An extensive bibliography is provided in Raymond Fielding's *Technique of Special Effects Cinematography* (3d ed., New York: Focal Press, 1972).

Youngblood, G. *Expanded Cinema.* See no. FC26.

Underground Film

Film-Makers' Cooperative Catalogue No. 6. See no. ED6.

FC25. *A History of the American Avant-Garde Cinema.* New York: American Federation of Arts, 1976.

An exhibition catalog, with these valuable reference features: chronology of independent film from 1943 through 1972; filmographies of 28 major independent filmmakers; bibliography. Not indexed.

FC26. Renan, Sheldon. *An Introduction to the American Underground Film.* New York: E. P. Dutton, 1967.

Guide to underground film. "Gallery of Film-makers" provides biographical information. Appendix names sources for renting films; lists important films and filmmakers. Indexed. Paperback edition.

Can be updated by P. Adams Sitney's *Visionary Film, The American Avant Garde* (New York: Oxford University Press, 1974) and Stephen Dwoskin's *Film is. . . The International Free Cinema* (London: Peter Owen, 1975). Both books index names and film titles.

Expanded Cinema, by Gene Youngblood (New York: E. P. Dutton, 1970), examines the new methods of creating an image: computer films, cybernetic cinema, cathode-ray tube videotronics, closed-circuit television, cable television, computer-generated holograms, and so on. Indexed. Available in paperback.

Westerns

FC27. Eyles, Allen. *The Western.* South Brunswick and New York: A. S. Barnes and Co., Inc., 1975.

Dictionary of names associated with Westerns: performers, directors, writers, cameramen, composers, actual historical figures. Complete through summer 1974. Index to film titles gives year of release. British changes of title are cross-referenced.

FC28. Fenin, George N., and Everson, William K. *The Western: From Silents to the Seventies.* New, expanded edition. New York: Grossman Publishers, 1973.

History of the Western movie. Fenin expands 1962 edition, subtitled "From Silents to Cinerama," with two chapters, one on Italian- and Japanese-made Westerns, the other on the last decade. Well illustrated. Index. Available in paperback (Penguin, 1977).

FC29. Hembus, Joe. *Western-Lexikon. 1272 Filme von 1894–1975.* Munich: Carl Hanser, 1976.

Detailed encyclopedia of Westerns; international in coverage. Arranged by German version of title. Gives: title in original language, principal cast, brief summary of action, comment. Index to original title refers to German-language entry. Bibliography of Western film literature. Index to names and characters.

FC30. Nachbar, John G. *Western Films: An Annotated Critical Bibliography.* New York: Garland Publishing, 1975.

Cites serious criticism of Western films. Does not include reviews of specific films or fan magazine articles. Arranged by broad topics, each section is subdivided into books and articles. Entries are briefly described with cross-references where necessary. Limited to English-language sources. Lists periodicals that deal with filmed westerns. Indexes: author, subject.

FC31. Parish, James R., and Pitts, Michael R. *The Great Western Pictures.* Edited by T. Allan Taylor. Metuchen, N.J.: Scarecrow Press, 1976.

Describes Westerns produced in U.S., with few European additions. Names technical staff and cast, summarizes story, and adds comment. Includes series. Also: Western shows on radio and television, and bibliography of Western novels.

Women in Moving Pictures

Dawson, B. *Women's Films in Print.* See no. ED5.

Films by and/or about Women. See.no. ED7.

FC32. Haskell, Molly. *From Reverence to Rape; The Treatment of Women in Movies.* New York: Holt, Rinehart and Winston, 1974.
Important study of an important aspect of film. Includes chapter on European treatment of women in film. Illustrated with stills. Index. Available in paperback.

FC33. Kowalski, Rosemary R. *Women and Film: A Bibliography.* Metuchen, N.J.: Scarecrow Press, 1976.
Arranged in four sections: women as performers, as filmmakers, as columnists and critics, and images of women. Includes articles and books; introduction defines coverage. Subject index.

FC34. Smith, Sharon. *Women Who Make Movies.* New York: Hopkinson and Blake, 1975.
History and directory of women filmmakers. Discusses women in Hollywood, including screenwriters, editors, etc., since 1896; then women around the world, by country. Describes work of almost 90 American filmmakers outside Hollywood. Directory of women filmmakers throughout the U.S. gives address, lists productions, and, for some, refers to discussion in text. Also directories of organizations and distributors. Brief bibliography. Illustrated; index. Available in paperback.

FD. Basic Studies of Theory and Technique

These books are basic to the history of moving pictures. The section is arranged in two parts: studies of theory and aesthetics and studies of technique.

The *Basic Studies of Theory and Aesthetics* (nos. FD1 through FD11) are important for an understanding of the art of the film. Several also offer other reference features, such as filmographies and bibliographies.

Any list such as this is open to debate; admittedly it is a personal selection. But this list can easily be expanded with a library card catalog, under the subject heading: Moving Pictures.

Theory and Aesthetics

FD1. Arnheim, Rudolph. *Film as Art.* Berkeley: University of California Press, 1957.
One of the classic works on film theory. Most important for its discussion of silent film. Paperback edition.

FD2. Balazs, Bela. *Theory of the Film: Character and Growth of a New Art.* Translated by Edith Bone. New York: Dover Publications, 1971.

A classic contribution to theory and aesthetics of film art. Illustrated; index. First published in English in 1952. Paperback edition. Also reprinted by Arno Press (1972).

FD3. Bluestone, George. *Novels into Film.* Berkeley: University of California Press, 1957.

Discusses aesthetic and practical considerations of adapting a novel into film. Surveys similar and dissimilar characteristics, then analyzes six novels that have been filmed. Selected bibliography. Index. Paperback edition.

FD4. Bobker, Lee R. *Elements of Film.* 2d ed. New York: Harcourt Brace Jovanovich, 1974.

Compact introduction to film technique and aesthetics. Bobker, a filmmaker himself, discusses story and script, image, sound, and editing, then describes art of director and performer. Final section on film criticism. Most chapters conclude with supplementary reading. Paperback edition.

FD5. Eisenstein, Sergei. *Film Form, Essays in Film Theory and The Film Sense.* Edited and translated by Jay Leyda. New York: Meridian Books, 1957.

Combines Eisenstein's two most important works available in English, both classics in film literature. Addressed to his fellow filmmakers and students, these essays elaborate his theories and analyze his technique. Bibliography at end of each work. Only *Film Form* is indexed. Following *Film Sense,* Leyda has provided filmography of Eisenstein's work, spanning 1920–47, and bibliography of his writings in English. *Film Sense* first published in U.S. in 1942 and revised in 1947; *Film Form* in 1949. Both available in paperback (Harcourt Brace Jovanovich).

FD6. Gessner, Robert. *The Moving Image: A Guide to Cinematic Literacy.* New York: E. P. Dutton, 1968.

Studies history and art of screenplay. Author describes this work as "cinematic dramaturgy, the process in script form that inaugurates the creation of the product." Illustrated with script segments, stills, charts. Excellent bibliography, pp. 409–19, with sections on aesthetics, directors (monographs), general history, production, scripts, and periodicals; not annotated. Glossary of terms and list of sources for film rental. Index. Available in paperback.

FD7. Lawson, John Howard. *Film: The Creative Process; The Search for an Audio-Visual Language and Structure.* 2d ed. Preface by Jay Leyda. New York: Hill & Wang, 1967.
Examines art and theory of filmmaking. The author, a screenwriter, discusses principles of language, theory, and structure. Useful bibliography, pp. 361–68. Illustrated; index. Paperback edition.

FD8. Lindgren, Ernest. *The Art of the Film.* 2d ed. New York: Macmillan, 1963.
Important introduction to principles of film technique, with emphasis on aesthetics and theory. Concludes with section on film criticism. Selected bibliography and glossary. Illustrated; index. Available in paperback (1970).

FD9. Nicoll, Allardyce. *Film and Theatre.* New York: T. Y. Crowell Co., 1936. (Reprinted: Arno Press, 1972.)
Relates art of the stage to artistic principles of film. Old now, but still valuable for its bibliography, pp. 195–241, and eight-page list of periodicals. Neither list is annotated, but they were probably the most comprehensive bibliographies to that date.

FD10. Pudovkin, V. I. *Film Technique and Film Acting.* Translated and edited by Ivor Montagu. New York: Grove Press, 1970.
Two works published together. *Film Technique* covers practical filmmaking; *Film Acting* aims to dissociate film actors from theater style and guides them in the process. A critical filmography of Pudovkin's work concludes this edition. *Pudovkin on Film Technique* was first published in English in 1929 and *Film Acting* in 1937, yet they both remain basic to any philosophy of film art. Paperback edition.

FD11. Vardac, A. N. *Stage to Screen: Theatrical Method from Garrick to Griffith.* Cambridge, Mass.: Harvard University Press, 1949. (Reprinted: Arno Press, 1968.)
Studies aesthetic merger of stage and screen. Notes, pp. 255–69, suggest some excellent primary sources for film research, such as promptbooks, periodical accounts of productions, moving picture catalogs. Index.

Technique

The *Basic Studies of Technique* (nos. FD12 through FD19) provide background and information about the technical side of moviemaking. The handiest, most reliable source is probably Spottiswoode's *Focal Encyclopedia of Film and Television Techniques* (no. B21). Books listed in this section offer detail about particular aspects of technique. Several include glossaries of terms and bibliographies for further study.

American Cinematographer Manual. See no. B4.

FD12. Baddeley, W. Hugh. *The Technique of Documentary Film Production.* Library of Communication Techniques. 4th rev. ed. New York: Hastings House, 1975.

Guide to production of factual films, from preparation of script to distribution. Includes such aspects as lighting, editing, sound. Glossary of terms. Index. Available in paperback.

FD13. Brodbeck, Emil E. *Handbook of Basic Motion-Picture Techniques.* 2d ed. New York: Prentice-Hall, 1975.

A simply presented guide, frequently used as classroom text. This edition adds chapter on more advanced principles and techniques. Illustrated; index.

Focal Encyclopedia of Film and Television Techniques. See no. B21.

FD14. Mascelli, Joseph V. *The Five C's of Cinematography: Motion Picture Filming Techniques Simplified.* 7th ed. Hollywood: Cine/Grafic Publications, 1977.

A manual for the filmmaker, covering camera angle, continuity, cutting, close-ups, composition. Combines full explanation with abundant illustrations. Index. Apparently a reissue of original 1965 edition.

FD15. Reisz, Karel, and Millar, Gavin. *The Technique of Film Editing.* Library of Communication Techniques. 2d enl. ed. New York: Hastings House, 1968.

Discusses history, craft, and principles of film editing. Includes brief bibliography, glossary of terms, section on cutting-room procedure. This edition includes addenda by Thorold Dickinson. Available in paperback.

FD16. Roberts, Kenneth H., and Sharples, Jr., Win. *A Primer for*

Filmmaking: A Complete Guide to 16mm and 35mm Film Production. New York: Pegasus, 1971.

Technical guide to filmmaking—covers camera, lighting, editing, laboratory, opticals and titles, sound, and budgeting. Extremely detailed and complete; aimed at both professional filmmakers and students of film. Also lists necessary equipment; film rental catalogs and companies; nomenclature; brief annotated bibliography. Illustrated; index. Available in paperback.

FD17. Spottiswoode, Raymond. *Film and its Technique.* Berkeley: University of California Press, 1952.

Standard work on film technique; still consulted despite its 1952 imprint date. Explains technical processes of filmmaking, from script to screen. Includes glossary and annotated list of books, pp. 485–501. Illustrated; indexes: film titles, general.

FD18. Swain, Dwight V. *Film Scriptwriting: A Practical Manual.* Communication Arts Books. New York: Hastings House, 1976.

Guides one through essentials of writing a feature or a fact film. Useful section of "lessons from the pros." Bibliography, pp. 352–55, and list of terms. Indexed.

Two other important books on this topic: John Howard Lawson, *Theory and Technique of Playwriting and Screenwriting* (New York: Hill & Wang, 1960) and Norton S. Parker, *Audiovisual Script Writing* (New Brunswick, N.J.: Rutgers University Press, 1968).

FD19. Wheeler, Leslie J. *Principles of Cinematography: A Handbook of Motion Picture Technology.* 4th ed. New York: International Publications Service, 1973.

Deals with mechanics of cinematography—theory and purpose of camera, printer, projector, etc. Excellent bibliography (pp. 383–429) groups books, pamphlets, journals articles by subjects. Illustrated; index. U.S. release of British 4th edition (London: Fountain Press, 1969).

G. Biography

Biographies provide personal information about people involved with moving pictures. Some of the books included here are encyclopedic in nature and provide filmographies and even bibliographies for each individual; for example, *Notable Names in the American Theatre* (no. G8), the *World Encyclopedia of the Film* (no. G17), and *Filmlexicon degli autori* (no. G4), the master work of its type.

A few titles given here are subjective collections of comments by film scholars, such as Sadoul's *Dictionary of Film Makers* (no. G13), Thomson's *Biographical Dictionary of Film* (no. G18), and Ford's *Dictionnaire des cinéastes* (no. G6). Each is worth consulting—opinions and all—because of facts they provide or up-to-date information. Plus they make interesting reading!

Some books in this section index other sources of information about people, for example, *Biography Index* (no. G3), *New York Times Obituaries Index* (no. G9), and Schuster's *Motion Picture Directors* (no. G14) and *Motion Picture Performers* (nos. G15 and G16).

This guide does not cite monographs on directors or performers—hundreds, perhaps thousands, of these have been published. They can be located by the subject's name in card catalogs or in bookstores.

Biographical information can also be found in abundance in dictionaries and encyclopedias (Section B) and in the who's who section of annuals and directories (Section C).

G1. Academy of Motion Picture Arts and Sciences. *Academy Players Directory*. Los Angeles: AMPAS, 1937– .

Photographic gallery of performers, grouped by type (e.g., leading women and men, ingenues, characters and comedians, etc.). Published for casting purposes, but can aid in identifying performers.

Another identification aid is *"Who is That?" The Late Late Viewers*

Guide to the Old Old Movie Players, by Warren B. Meyers (New York: Personality Posters, 1967. Reprint: Citadel Press, 1976). Groups performers by type, such as: the other woman, motherly types, bad guys, ethnic types, etc. Index to all names.

G2. Bellour, Raymond, and Brochier, Jean-Jacques, eds. *Dictionnaire du cinéma.* Paris: Éditions Universitaires, 1966.
  Biographical dictionary of world's major directors, scriptwriters, and producers. International in coverage, but emphasis on France. Each article provides brief vita, filmography, bibliography, and critical opinion signed by an expert. Illustrated. Index to names cited.

Bessy, M., and Chardans, J-L. *Dictionnaire du cinéma et de la télévision.* See no. B2.

Bibliographie internationale cinéma. See no. DB3.

G3. *Biography Index.* New York: H. W. Wilson Co., 1947–.
  Indexes biographical material that has appeared in books, some 1,500 journals (including foreign), and important obituaries from *New York Times;* also analyzes collective biographies. Alphabetical listing of names. Quarterly, with annual and three-year cumulations.

Birkos, A. S. *Soviet Cinema: Directors and Films.* See no. FB31.

British Film and Television Year Book. See no. CA5.

Bucher F. *Germany.* See no. FB15.

Enciclopedia dello spettacolo. See nos. B6, B7 and B8.

G4. *Filmlexicon degli autori e delle opere.* 7 vols. Rome: Bianco e Nero, 1958–67. (In progress.)
  Sponsored by Centro Sperimentale di Cinematografia. International in coverage. Introduction in Italian, French, English, German, and Spanish; text in Italian. First seven volumes, "Autori," list people involved in the creative activity of moving pictures: directors, screenwriters, producers, performers, cameramen, composers, art directors, costume designers—for both silent and sound film. Entries provide: biographical sketches; filmographies, which name films in original language and in Italian and give principals and dates; and bibliographies, based mostly on Italian publications. Greatly expands Pasinetti's *Filmlexicon* (see no. B17).

Volumes are planned that will deal with films ("Opere"). They will give detailed plot synopsis, historical-critical comment, and international bibliography. Also projected: a dictionary, biographical directory of film historians and essayists, general index to all films mentioned.

G5. ———. *Autori aggiornamenti 1958–1971.* 2 vols. Rome: Bianco e Nero, 1973–74.

Updates original set, above, with recent information on names previously cited and with new additions.

G6. Ford, Charles. *Dictionnaire des cinéastes contemporains, de 1945 à nos jours.* Verviers, Belgium: Marabout université, 1974.

Compiled for casual reference, not scholarly detail. Covers filmmakers whose work has been seen in Western Europe since 1945. Each entry states background of director, producer, or screenwriter; gives brief appraisal by Ford; lists films made since 1945, along with major cast. Film titles are generally given in original language, although sometimes a literal translation in French is used.

Graham, P. *A Dictionary of the Cinema.* See no. B11.

International Motion Picture Almanac. "Who's Who in Motion Pictures and Television." See no. CA14.

G7. Lamparski, Richard. *Whatever Became of . . . ?* New York: Crown Publishers, 1967–.

This series follows up on the careers of movie personalities. Index to names and film titles. Also published in Bantam Book paperback editions.

Leprohon, P. *The Italian Cinema.* See no. FB21.

Leyda, J. *Dianying: An Account of Films and the Film Audience in China.* See no. FB2.

Martin, M. *France.* See no. FB13.

G8. McGill, Raymond D., *Notable Names in the American Theatre.* Clifton, N. J.: James T. White & Co., 1976.

New, second edition of *Biographical Encyclopedia & Who's Who of the American Theater,* edited by Walter Rigdon (New York: James H. Heineman, 1966). Brief biographical information about people active in American theater, followed by credits for work in theater, films, television, radio. Also lists awards and publications. A Necrology gives birth and death dates.

Both editions should be used, because the second edition deletes some names that were included in the first. Future volumes are planned to emphasize careers in film, television, music, and dance.

Michael, P. *The American Movies Reference Book.* See no. B14.

G9. *New York Times Obituaries Index: 1858–1968.* New York: New York Times, 1970.

Provides access to biographies of many film people by giving date of obituary in *New York Times.* One can then locate story in other publications or newspapers such as *Los Angeles Times, London Times.* Brings together, in a single alphabetical listing, over 353,000 names. Update with the *New York Times Index;* consult the heading "Deaths." *Facts on File* (see no. IC12) indexes obituaries more quickly.

G10. Ragan, David. *Who's Who in Hollywood 1900–1976.* New Rochelle, N.Y.: Arlington House Publishers, 1976.

Dictionary of several thousand screen performers, including international performers seen in American releases. Arranged in two sections: living players, which names major moving picture credits; and late players, 1900–1974, which includes year of death, age at death, and significant films. Also lists performers who died in 1975 and 1976, "lost" players and "lost" child players. Amount of information for each entry varies considerably.

G11. Reichow, Joachim. *Filmkünstler A–Z.* Leipzig: VEB Bibliographisches Institut, 1967.

International listing of performers, directors, cameramen, documentary filmmakers, screenwriters. Provides brief biography and filmography—unfortunately all films are given in German translation. Useful for elusive German and East European film people.

Another similar book: *Wir vom Film* by Charles Reinert (Basel: Herder Freiburg, 1960), gives short biographies for 1,300 international performers, directors, writers, etc. and lists films of each in language of origin.

G12. Reichow, Joachim, and Hanisch, Michael. *Filmschauspieler A–Z.* Berlin: Henschel-Verlag, 1971.

Directory of international film stars—living and dead. Entry provides brief biography along with list of films. Film titles are given in original language, with release date. Bibliography.

Rondolino, G. *Dizionario del cinema italiano.* See no. FB23.

G13. Sadoul, Georges. *Dictionary of Film Makers.* Translated, edited, and updated by Peter Morris. Berkeley: University of California Press, 1972.

Identifies persons other than performers involved with film industry. Emphasizes directors, but includes scenarists, cameramen, designers, animators, musicians, film writers, inventors, etc., and names their principal works. International in coverage, although emphasis is on European names. Real value is in comments of this famous film scholar. Illustrated. Expands the original *Dictionnaire des cinéastes* (Paris: Éd. du Seuil, 1965), which provided excellent section not in translation: "Repertoire des films" (filmography) by country; "Bio-filmographies d'auteurs," which cites monographs on individual directors; and lists of film histories, both international and by country. Unfortunately, there is no cross-referencing between this volume and its companion, *Dictionary of Films* (see no. EA11). Available in paperback.

G14. Schuster, Mel, comp. *Motion Picture Directors: A Bibliography of Magazine and Periodical Articles, 1900–1972.* Metuchen, N.J.: Scarecrow Press, 1973.

Follows his *Motion Picture Performers* (see below). Over 300 magazines, both film and general, were scanned for this work. Provides a list of directors for whom no material was found. Arranged by director or filmmaker. Limited to English-language publications.

G15. Schuster, Mel, comp. *Motion Picture Performers: A Bibliography of Magazine and Periodical Articles, 1900–1969.* Metuchen, N.J.: Scarecrow Press, 1971.

Cites articles about moving picture performers from more than 150 English-language popular journals. Coverage: 1900 to mid-1969. Magazine supplements of some newspapers included; generally excludes fan magazines, except those of the teens and 1920s. Arranged alphabetically by performer; includes list of performers for whom no material was found. Continued by:

G16. ———. *Motion Picture Performers: A Bibliography of Magazine and Periodical Articles; Supplement 1, 1970–1974.* Metuchen, N.J.: Scarecrow Press, 1976.

Greatly expands the basic volume. Updates through 1974, adding 2,600 performers for a total of 5,500 in the set. Adds more periodicals, including film journals and some fan magazines, for a total of 300 that are indexed. Arranged alphabetically by performer; citations given chronologically. Many gaps in the earlier volume are filled. Pertinent entries from the *Cumulated Dramatic Index 1909–1949* are included. (Note: the *Dramatic Index*, no. IC2, covered fan magazines, just about the only moving picture literature in the early days.)

Screen World. See no. CA20.

G17. Smith, John M., and Cawkwell, Tim, eds. *The World Encyclopedia of the Film.* New York: World Publishing, 1972.

Biographies with film lists for over 2,000 artists who have worked in film: directors, performers, producers, writers, technicians, composers. International in coverage. Illustrated. Index to all films listed in biographical entries—20,000 films in all—with cross-references to variant titles or titles in original language. Index also gives, for each title: date, credits, literary source, studio, physical features. Result is an extremely useful international filmography. Available in paperback (A & W Visual Library, 1975).

Svensson, A. *Japan.* See no. FB26.

G18. Thomson, David. *A Biographical Dictionary of Film.* New York: Wm. Morrow & Co., 1976.

A collection of critical essays on over 800 directors, performers, producers. Arranged alphabetically by name. Suggests further reading. One may disagree with opinions of the author, but this dictionary does supply up-to-date information. First published in England as: *A Biographical Dictionary of the Cinema* (1975). Available in paperback.

G19. Truitt, Evelyn Mack, comp. *Who Was Who on Screen.* 2d ed. New York: R. R. Bowker, 1977.

Biographical information for 9,000 screen personalities, mostly American, British, and French, who died between 1905 and 1976. Arranged alphabetically by name. Each entry provides vital statistics, awards, complete list of screen credits—when available. Includes stars, supporting and bit players, stuntpeople, animal stars, and celebrities from other fields who have appeared on screen.

G20. Twomey, Alfred E., and McClure, Arthur F. *The Versatiles.* South Brunswick and New York: A.S. Barnes and Co., Inc., 1969.

Subtitled: "A Study of Supporting Character Actors and Actresses in the American Motion Picture, 1930–1955." Biographical dictionary divided into two sections. First section lists performers about whom considerable information was available; second, those for whom few facts could be found. Both sections provide filmography. Illustrated; no index. A sequel, *Character People,* is in preparation.

Winchester, C. *The World Film Encyclopedia.* See no. B23.

H. Film Reviews and Criticism

There are various ways to locate reviews of moving pictures. Samples's *How to Locate Reviews of Plays and Films* (no. H9) suggests many approaches.

Bowles's *Index to Critical Film Reviews* (no. H2) and Salem's *Guide to Critical Reviews* (no. H8) cite reviews that have appeared in periodicals. Although they appear to be similar, it is worth noting that Bowles indexes scholarly film journals and covers a greater period of time (1930–72). Salem indexes general periodicals, covers 1927–63, and includes more film titles.

The *Monthly Film Bulletin* (no. H3), *Film Review Digest* (no. H4), *Filmfacts* (no. H5), and the *New York Times Film Reviews* (no. H7) furnish the review itself, or part of it.

This guide does not cite works by individual critics, because these are easily located in a card catalog or in a bookstore by the critic's name. One can also consult the subject heading Moving Pictures—Reviews in the card catalog. The *Subject Guide to Books in Print* (no. DB6) lists books "dealing with the concept and technique of moving picture reviews" under Moving Picture Criticism.

Several collections of film criticism that offer historical coverage are cited at the end of this section, but general anthologies are not included. Heinzkill's *Film Criticism* (no. H6) serves as an excellent index to information in the standard collections of criticism.

Most periodical indexes (Section IC) list film reviews and are the best place to look for reviews of *current* moving pictures.

H1. Amberg, George. *The New York Times Film Reviews, a One-Volume Selection, 1913–1970.* New York: Quadrangle, 1972.

Four hundred reviews, chosen from the six-volume set (see no. H7), and arranged by date. Title index.

H2. Bowles, Stephen E., comp. and ed. *Index to Critical Film*

Reviews in British and American Film Periodicals. 3 vols. in 2. New York: Burt Franklin. 1974–75.

Title continues: "Together with Index to Critical Reviews of Books about Film." Divided into two sections; first: cites over 20,000 film reviews published in 31 periodicals, from first issue to termination, or through 1971 (when annual *International Index to Film Periodicals* begins; see no. IC6). Arranged by film title. Citation includes reviewer's name when known; whether full, partial, or no credits are given; script excerpts. Second section cites over 6,000 reviews of books about film; arranged by title of book. These indexes conclude vol. 3: directors, film reviewers, authors, book reviewers, subject index to books. Union list of periodicals, pp. 767–73, gives locations in American and Canadian libraries of cited periodicals.

H3. British Film Institute. *Monthly Film Bulletin.* London: 1934–. Monthly.

Edited by Richard Combs. Each issue briefly reviews 40 to 60 feature films and several short films. International in coverage. Films arranged alphabetically by title in original language, with full credits. Table of contents on front cover. Annual index lists feature films, nonfiction and short films, feature directors.

Film Daily Year Book of Motion Pictures. "Features Released since 1915" refers to review date in *Film Daily.* See no. CA10.

H4. *Film Review Digest.* Millwood, N.Y.: Kraus-Thomson Organization, Fall, 1975–. Quarterly.

Digests film reviews from over two dozen American, Canadian, and British periodicals. Includes film journals; newspapers such as *Los Angeles Times, New York Times, Village Voice*; and several weekly magazines (the *New Yorker* and *Variety* are not included). Aims to cover all feature films presented to American audiences each year—including Bs. Information given: full credits, running time, year of production, country and original name for foreign films. Extracts from one to five paragraphs of a review. Indexes: film titles and casts; reviewers. Also useful as an index to film reviews.

The reviews that appeared in Vol. 1 (fall and winter 1975, spring and summer 1976) have been cumulated in the *Film Review Digest Annual 1976,* edited by David M. Brownstone and Irene M. Franck (Millwood, N.Y.: KTO Press, 1976). Arranged alphabetically by film title. Section on awards. General index to all names and film titles; separate index to critics.

H5. *Filmfacts.* Los Angeles: University of Southern California, 1958–.
Edited by Ernest Parmentier. Reviews 10 to 15 films in each issue; international in coverage. Gives full credits, synopsis, critique, extracts from reviews in journals and newspapers by well-known critics. No contents page, but indexed annually. Has a complicated history: volumes for 1964, 1965, 1969, 1973 are incomplete; never published in 1970; 1974 and 1975 are planned; 1976 is in progress.

H6. Heinzkill, Richard. *Film Criticism: An Index to Critics' Anthologies.* Metuchen, N.J.: Scarecrow Press, 1975.
Indexes 40 anthologies of film criticism, many of which do not have their own index. It cites—in one alphabet—names of performers and directors and film and book titles that are mentioned in the texts. Includes mostly American works and a few British.

New York Times Directory of the Film. See no. CB9.

H7. *The New York Times Film Reviews, 1913–1968.* 5 vols. and *Appendix/Index.* New York: Arno Press, 1970.
———, *1969–1974.* 3 vols. New York: Arno Press, 1972–76.
Main set reprints more than 16,000 film reviews, published in *New York Times* from 1913 through 1968. Arranged chronologically; each item cites date and page of review. Illustrations also reproduced. Feature and news articles pertaining to film incorporated in first two volumes; only daily reviews in next three volumes, excluding the lengthy Sunday articles. Before 1913, the *Times* treated movies as curiosities; until late 1924, reviews were anonymous.
Vol. 6, *Appendix/Index 1913–1968,* includes: Addenda, which corrects erroneous citations and adds reviews omitted from first five volumes; Awards, including the *Times* "ten best" since 1924, New York Film Critics Circle Awards since 1935, and Academy Awards since 1927; Portrait Gallery of about 2,000 movie stars. Index divided into three main parts: titles, persons, and corporations. Persons Index lists every performer, producer, director, screenwriter, etc. mentioned in reviews, giving credits in chronological order. The Corporation Index lists producing,

distributing, and participating companies. A similar version of this volume is available as the *New York Times Directory of the Film* (see no. CB9).

Three supplements reprint about 6,000 daily reviews, from January 1, 1969, through December 31, 1974, as well as Sunday "think pieces." Vol. 7, 1969–70, includes errata to 1913–68 set. Each volume indexed. An ongoing publication. A volume for the years 1975-76 is in preparation.

Consult *Index* to the *New York Times* for film reviews after 1974. See heading "Motion pictures" with its myriad subdivisions. Reviews of individual films listed by title under "Motion Pictures—Reviews and Other Data on Specific Productions." Runs about two months behind.

H8. Salem, James M. *A Guide to Critical Reviews.* Part 4: *The Screenplay from "The Jazz Singer" to "Dr. Strangelove."* 2 vols. Metuchen, N.J.: Scarecrow Press, 1971.

Cites critical reviews of about 12,000 American and foreign feature-length films released from October 1927 through 1963. Films arranged alphabetically by title. Reviews are from popular American and Canadian periodicals and the *New York Times;* does not include critical articles from scholarly journals. Films released under various titles are cross-referenced. Based on Dimmitt's *Title Guide to the Talkies* (see no. EF1), with some additions.

Part 2: *The Musical, 1909–1974* (1976), in this series, covers the musical on New York stage. Its indexes are useful here, particularly of authors, composers, and lyricists; and titles and authors of original source (including movies). The other two parts of this series do the same thing for stage plays.

H9. Samples, Gordon. *How to Locate Reviews of Plays and Films; a Bibliography of Criticism from the Beginnings to the Present.* Metuchen, N.J.: Scarecrow Press, 1976.

Second part of book lists sources that review films. Arranged chronologically by dates of films that are covered. Sections: study guides that discuss or list films; review indexing services; newspaper indexes; cinema criticism checklists; collected reviews of individual critics; leading film periodicals; documentary and factual film guides; special effects and animated film guides; reference guides; representative film distributors' catalogs; sources for stills. Each entry is described. Index to authors and titles.

Writer's Program. New York. *The Film Index.* See no. DA15.

H10. These collections of film criticism are included because of their historical coverage and reference value. All titles are indexed.

Denby, David, ed. *Awake in the Dark: An Anthology of American Film Criticism, 1915 to the Present.* New York: Vintage Books, 1977. (Paperback edition)

Film . . . : An Anthology by the National Society of Film Critics. 1968–. An annual anthology of American film criticism. *Film 67/68, 68/69, 69/70, 70/71, 71/72* published by Simon and Schuster (New York). *Film 72/73, 73/74* published by Bobbs-Merrill (Indianapolis).

Hochman, Stanley, comp. and ed. *American Film Directors.* A Library of Film Criticism. New York: Frederick Ungar Publ. Co., 1974.

Kauffmann, Stanley, ed. *American Film Criticism, from the Beginnings to "Citizen Kane." Reviews of Significant Films at the Time They First Appeared.* With Bruce Henstell. New York: Liveright, 1972.

I. Periodicals

Much of the important work in film studies can be found in periodicals. Most provide articles on specific aspects of film, as well as filmographies and bibliographies, reviews of feature and special films, book reviews, interviews, current events. They can be considered supplements to the more formal—and dated—books in this guide. The reference features of journals are enhanced when they have an index or are indexed elsewhere.

IA. Selection of Important Film Periodicals

Hundreds and hundreds of film periodicals are published in this world, and this list of twelve is indeed a selection. Special features of these major periodicals from the United States, Canada, England, France, and Italy are briefly described.

A few have their own index; e.g., *L'avant-scène, Bianco e nero, Film Comment, Films in Review*. Several of the others are indexed in general periodical indexes (Section IC, nos. IC9–IC18). Almost all of them are indexed in the film periodical indexes (Section IC, nos. IC1–IC8).

Many film buffs consider the British *Sight and Sound* (no. IA9) to be the best film journal. *Film Comment, Film Culture, Film Quarterly,* and the weekly *Variety* are among the popular American periodicals.

IA1. *L'Avant-scène du cinéma*. Paris: 1961–. Monthly (except August).

Each issue publishes full shooting script of a popular feature film. Text in French, despite film's origin. Includes signed critical essay, full credits, movie stills, extracts of reviews from French press, and, occasionally, bio-filmographies for stars or director. Issue no. 109 (December 1970) has "Table alphabetique des films" that indexes feature and short films discussed since Issue 1 (1961–70). More recent issues have summaries on outside back cover. Also indexed through 1972 in Samples's *Drama Scholars' Index to Plays and Filmscripts* (see no. EE9). *International Film Guide* (see no. CA13) lists contents each year in "Film Magazines" section.

IA2. *Bianco e nero.* Rome: Centro sperimentale di cinematografia, 1937–. Bimonthly.

Italy's leading film journal. Each issue interviews a film personality; lists festivals and exhibits; reviews films; lists, with full credits, films appearing in Rome. Some issues extract a screenplay, in original language. General index each year to subjects, writers, films, and directors. Theatrical productions and directors are also indexed.

British Film Institute. *Monthly Film Bulletin.* See no. H3.

IA3. *Cahiers du cinéma.* Evreux, France: 1951–. Monthly.

Leading French film journal. Articles on directors, screenwriters, films, festivals, national cinema. Includes filmographies of directors. Separate index for issues 1 through 100 (October 1959). No. 101 (November 1959) and after have a summary on inside front cover of each issue. Format and contents vary. A regular feature is "Films sortis à Paris," which describes films shown in Paris during previous month.

IA4. *Film Comment.* New York: 1962–. Bimonthly.

Currently edited by Richard Corliss. Articles on individuals, national styles, and interviews often include filmographies. Has been indexed annually since 1972 (vol. 8). Spring 1970 issue (vol. 6, no. 1) gives complete contents for all earlier issues. Also indexed in *Humanities Index.*

IA5. *Film Culture.* New York: 1955–. Quarterly.

Currently edited by Jonas Mekas. Has become voice of avant-garde. Includes articles on recent developments; essays on art; signed reviews of films, domestic and foreign; book reviews; technical data; film indexes. "Books Received" section. Indexed in *Art Index.*

IA6. *Film Quarterly.* Berkeley: University of California Press, 1945–. Quarterly.

Currently edited by Ernest Callenbach. Scholarly journal; has feature articles, lengthy signed film reviews (about five per issue), brief discussion of two to fifteen other films, and book reviews.

Annual index to film and book titles, names, and major topics. Earlier titles: *Hollywood Quarterly* (1945–Summer 1951) and *Quarterly of Film, Radio and Television* (Fall 1951–Summer 1957). Vols. 4 through 11 (1949–Summer 1957) had regular "Bibliography for the Quarter," which described new publications, including books, catalogs, reports, pamphlets, and journals. Indexed in *Readers' Guide, Art Index,* and *Humanities Index.*

Filmfacts. See no. H5.

IA7. *Films and Filming.* London: 1954–. Monthly.

Currently edited by Robin Bean. Regularly features "Filmguide," which names British releases, with dates and rating. Also provides essays; 10 to 20 signed film reviews; and "World Production Guide," grouped by country. Not indexed.

IA8. *Films in Review.* New York: National Board of Review of Motion Pictures, 1950–. Monthly/bimonthly in summer.

Currently edited by Charles P. Reilly. Most useful for articles on film personalities, with impressive filmography and movie stills. Indexed in *Art Index.*

The National Board of Review has published three indexes to *Films in Review:* vol. 1, 1950–59, and vol. 2, 1960–64, edited by Marion Fawcett (1961 and 1966); vol. 3, 1965–69, edited by Sandra Lester (1972).

Preceded by *New Movies* (New York, 1926–48, vols. 1–24), which is indexed in *A Film Students Index to the National Board of Review Magazine, 1926–1948*, by Nancy Warfield (Published by the author: 1974).

IA9. *Sight and Sound.* London: British Film Institute, 1932–. Quarterly.

Currently edited by Penelope Houston. Highly regarded film journal. Each issue includes articles, signed film reviews (generally about 10), signed book reviews. "Film Guide" rates films by four-star method and is probably the most quoted rating guide. Annual index to contributors, names, film titles, illustrations. Has changed format and emphasis considerably during the years. Originally concerned with film as an educational medium but changed gradually to treat film as art. Contributors have always been important critics and historians. Indexed in *Art Index, British Humanities Index, Humanities Index.*

IA10. *SMPTE Journal.* New York: Society of Motion Picture and Television Engineers, 1916–. Monthly.
   Initially, *Journal of the Society of Motion Picture Engineers.* Articles on technical aspects of film production. Annual indexes cumulate every five years and serve as bibliography of cinematography. Index divided into such headings as acoustics; apparatus; biographical notes; books, booklets, and brochures; book reviews; cinematography; etc.

IA11. *Take One, The Film Magazine.* Montreal, Canada, 1966–. Bimonthly.
   Currently edited by Peter Lebensold. Canada's prime film journal. Articles on filmmakers and filmmaking. Film and book reviews.

IA12. *Variety.* New York: 1905–. Weekly.
   Voice of the entertainment business. Covers moving pictures, television films, radio, music, stage. "Pictures" section has news items, feature articles, business reports, detailed statistics. Charts 50 top-grossing films of previous week. Reviews include credits for cameraman, technical advisor, wardrobe supervisor, set decorator, and other behind-the-scenes artists. Indexed only in *Music Index.*

IB. Periodical Lists

These lists can give a film researcher detailed information about film periodicals—such as place and date of publication—which can be useful in verifying or correcting mysterious citations. Reviews and news can also be located in those periodicals which are not indexed anywhere, via the publication date.

Bowles, S. E. *An Approach to Film Study.* Periodical section groups nearly 160 titles by type; reviewing sources; general academic and scholarly; special interest; filmmaking and audiovisual; film teaching; professional and industry information; English-language journals from outside the U.S. and Britain; popular and exploitation; the arts—including film. See no. A1.

IB1. British Film Institute. *Periodical Holdings 1974.* Edited by Gillian Barrett. London: BFI, 1974.
   Alphabetical list of periodicals held by British Film Institute. Information given: country of origin and holdings of BFI (by date, not volume numbers). Does not provide debut of publica-

tion but does refer to earlier and later titles. Excludes annuals and periodicals treated as books. Index to periodicals by country. Pamphlet format.

IB2. *Cinemages SP-2.* Special Issue No. 2 (15 April 1957). New York.
Attempted to list all of the world's known film journals. Includes addresses of 1,151 titles. *Cinemages* was published 1955 to 1959 by Group for Film Study in New York.

IB3. Cinémathèque de Belgique. Brussels. *Répertoire mondial des périodiques cinématographiques.* 2d ed. Brussels: 1960.
Also cited: *World List of Film Periodicals and Serials.* Geographic list of 786 periodicals from 57 countries and territories. Includes journals, yearbooks, publications that are periodically brought up to date, and film-card services. Each entry gives full address, date of debut, size, and brief description. Explanatory note in French and English. Indexes: titles, subjects, countries.

Gottesman, R., and Geduld, H. M. *Guidebook to Film: An Eleven-in-One Reference.* See no. A3.

International Federation of Film Archives. *Catalogue collectif des livres et périodiques publiés avant 1914.* See no. DC2.

International Film Guide. "Film Magazines" section. See no. CA13.

International Index to Film Periodicals. List of periodicals indexed. See no. IC6.

International Motion Picture Almanac. "Publications on Motion Pictures." See no. CA14.

Monaco, J. *How to Read a Film.* Directory of important film journals in English. See no. A7.

Motion Pictures: A Catalog of Books, Periodicals, Screen Plays and Production Stills. See no. DC3.

New York (City). Public Library. Research Libraries. *Catalog of the Theatre and Drama Collections. Part II: Theatre Collection: Books on the Theatre.* Film journals listed under "Cinema—Periodicals." See no. DC4 and DC5.

Nicoll, A. *Film and Theatre.* "List of periodicals." See no. FD9.

IB4. Paris. Bibliothèque Nationale. Département des périodiques. *Catalogue des périodiques français et étrangers consacres au cinéma.* . . . Établi par Pierre Moulinier, sous la direction de Jean Prinet. Paris: Institut des Hautes Études Cinématographiques, 1969.

Title translates: Catalog of French and foreign periodicals devoted to the cinema, kept in periodical department of Bibliothèque Nationale. Arranges 768 film periodicals by type: scholarly, technical, association publications, illustrated, specialized, miscellaneous. French and foreign periodicals listed separately. Information given: date of debut (or first issue held by Bibliothèque Nationale), name of editor, place of publication. Alphabetic index to all titles.

IB5. Reilly, Adam, comp. *Current Film Periodicals in English.* Rev. ed. New York: Educational Film Library Assoc., 1972.

Lists about 190 film periodicals in the English language that were being published in 1972. Dated now—some titles have died, others have appeared—but still useful. Provides subscription information, description of editorial policy, writer's market. Basic current information can be found in *Ulrich's International Periodicals Directory,* below. Booklet format.

IB6. *Ulrich's International Periodicals Directory 1977–1978.* 17th ed. New York: R. R. Bowker, 1977.

"A Classified Guide to Current Periodicals, Foreign and Domestic." Groups current film magazines under heading "Motion Pictures." For each title gives: debut date, frequency, price, editor, address, whether it includes book and film reviews, how and where indexed, circulation. 17th edition lists approximately 425 film and film-related journals. Title and subject index. Supplemented by *Ulrich's Quarterly.*

IC. Periodical Indexes

Any research project requires periodicals for up-to-date information. Indexing services will help in locating this information. Almost all indexes are arranged by subject, and each entry will provide the name of the article, author, periodical title, date, issue and volume, paging.

Film Periodical Indexes

Five of the indexes to film periodicals described below have appeared in the last several years. While film students before 1973 had to scour many sources for information in film journals, the question suddenly became: Which index do I use?

Briefly: three of these new indexes cover periodical literature from the 1930s to the early 1970s: Batty's *Retrospective Index* (no. IC1), the Gerlachs' *Critical Index* (no. IC4), and MacCann and Perry's *New Film Index* (no. IC7). *The New Film Index* is the most inclusive, but lacks a useful index, and the Gerlachs' *Critical Index* has a complicated arrangement. Batty's *Retrospective Index* may be the easiest to use, but it indexes much fewer periodicals.

These retrospective indexes can be continued by two of the new indexes that list current writings: the *International Index to Film Periodicals* (no. IC6), which began coverage in 1972, and *Film Literature Index* (no. IC3), which began in 1973.

IC1. Batty, Linda. *Retrospective Index to Film Periodicals 1930–1971*. New York: R. R. Bowker, 1975.

Indexes 14 film journals, from their debut through 1971, and pertinent articles in the *Village Voice*. Limited to English-language titles. Arranged in three parts: reviews of individual films; film subjects; book review citations. Mentions if an article includes a bibliography, a filmography, or a script extract. Can be continued by *International Index to Film Periodicals* (see no. IC6).

Bowles, S. E. *Index to Critical Film Reviews in British and American Film Periodicals*. See no. H2.

IC2. *The Dramatic Index*. Boston: 1909–49. Annual.

Indexed American and British publications concerned with theater, including fan magazines: one of the few early sources for news about moving pictures. Books, articles, government publications, pamphlets covered. Consult individual names and heading "Moving Pictures." Has been collected as: *Cumulated Dramatic Index 1909–1949*. 2 vols. (Boston: G. K. Hall, 1965).

IC3. *Film Literature Index: A Quarterly Author-Subject Periodical Index to the International Literature of Film*. Albany, N.Y.: Filmdex/ SUNY, 1973– .

Also referred to as *Filmdex*. Edited by Vincent J. Aceto, Jane Graves, Fred Silva. Indexes about 135 film journals and over 100 general periodicals that present film material; international in coverage. Arranges names, titles, and subjects in one alphabet. Article entries indicate the presence of filmography, credits,. biographical data, interviews. Film title entries include director's name, original release date, original-lanaguage title. Reviews of books on film are listed together in one section. Very thorough, with clear format. Issued quarterly, with annual cumulation. Each issue runs about one year behind.

Film Review Digest. See no. H4.

Films in Review. Indexes. See no. IA8.

IC4. Gerlach, John C., and Gerlach, Lana. *The Critical Index: A Bibliography of Articles on Film in English, 1946–1973, Arranged by Names and Topics.* New York: Teachers College Press, 1974.

Indexes 22 English-language film journals. Arranged by names (directors, performers, etc.) and then by topics (see introduction for classification scheme). Also includes pertinent articles from 60 general and literary periodicals. Some entries are annotated if the title is not self-explanatory. "List of Magazine Abbreviations" gives a useful history of indexed periodicals. Computer-produced format. Author and film-title indexes. Available in paperback.

IC5. *Guide to the Performing Arts.* 1957–68. New York: Scarecrow Press, 1960–72. Annual.

Compiled by S. Yancey Belknap. Began as supplement to *Guide to the Musical Arts, 1953–1956.* Articles on film listed under heading "Moving Pictures." Emphasis on film music. Cites film and book reviews.

IC6. *International Index to Film Periodicals.* In association with the International Federation of Film Archives. 1973–. Annual.

Sometimes cited: *FIAF Index* (after French name of sponsor, Fédération Internationale des Archives du Film). Indexes articles and reviews that appeared during a year in approximately 75 film journals from around the world. Arranged by subject areas with large sections for individual films, biography, film history; also includes section of general reference material. Articles are annotated in English and indexed by subject, film title (in original language), and names. Reviews are indexed only by film titles. Individual-films section includes articles written about uncompleted films, unrealized scripts, and films not yet released. Here is given country of origin, director, year of production and of first public showing, variant titles.

The list of periodicals indexed provides an up-to-date directory of international film journals. Each volume varies a bit:

1972 Index, Karen Jones, ed. (New York: R. R. Bowker). Subject index concludes volume.

1973 Index, Michael Moulds, ed. (New York: R. R. Bowker). Author and subject index conclude volume.

1974 Index, Karen Jones, ed. (New York: St. Martin's Press). Three indexes: director, author, subject.

Some libraries subscribe to the FIAF Periodical Indexing Service, which is kept on cards until the *Index* is received.

IC7. MacCann, Richard Dyer, and Perry, Edward S. *The New Film Index, A Bibliography of Magazine Articles in English, 1930–1970.* New York: E. P. Dutton, 1975.

Intended to continue *The Film Index* (see no. DA15). Cites only magazine articles; does not include books or films, as does the earlier work. Indexes nearly 40 English-language film periodicals, as well as pertinent articles in about 50 general magazines. Most entries are briefly described. Arranged by broad topics, then chronologically by publication date. Biography section lists articles by and about directors, producers, performers. Does not include film reviews or book reviews, but does cite criticism that provides thorough analysis. Index to *authors* of articles only; it is therefore necessary to search for coverage of one director, performer, etc.

IC8. *Media Review Digest.* Ann Arbor, Mich.: Pierian Press, 1973/74–. Quarterly.

Indexes reviews of films, filmstrips, slides, transparencies, illustrations, etc. Moving pictures listed by title in Film section. Emphasis is on educational media, but it includes periodicals devoted to entertainment film. Indexes over 200 journals (in 1976). Issued quarterly with annual cumulations; subject indexes issued annually. Continues *Multi-Media Reviews Index* (1970–72).

A similar publication,*International Index to Multi-Media Information* (Pasadena, Calif.: Audio-Visual Associates, 1970–), indexes every sort of media: moving pictures, filmstrips, slides, video recordings, and audio recordings, and so on. The Access section lists film titles under "Motion Picture Reel"; full information is given in Title section: distributor, running time, purchase or rental price, audience appeal, references to published reviews. Emphasis is on education film, but feature films are included. Covers about 150 journals, 20 of which treat entertainment film.

Producer/distributor directory. Incorporates *Film Review Index.* Quarterly.

The New York Times Film Reviews. See no. H7.

Powers, A. *Blacks in American Movies.* See no. DA8.

Vincent, C.; Redi, R.; and Venturini, F. *General Bibliography of Motion Pictures.* See no. DA14.

Writer's Program. New York. *The Film Index.* See no. DA15.

General Indexes

These indexes will turn up articles in some film periodicals, but they are chiefly useful for locating articles about moving pictures in general and popular magazines. Many film students may find themselves in a library without any film periodical indexes, but almost every library will have the *Readers' Guide to Periodical Literature* (no. IC18). Most college or university libraries would have the *Humanities Index* (no. IC13) and possibly the *Art Index* (no. IC10).

IC9. *Alternative Press Index: An Index to Alternative and Underground Publications.* Northfield, Minn.: Radical Research Center, 1960–. Quarterly.

Subtitled: "An Index to the Publications which Amplify the Cry for Social Change and Social Justice." Films are listed by title under "Film Reviews." Also check individual names and general heading "Film" (which refers to other headings such as underground movies, film festivals, censorship). Runs about one and a half years late.

IC10. *Art Index: A Cumulative Author and Subject Index to a Selected List of Fine Art Periodicals.* New York: H. W. Wilson Co., 1929–

Indexes American and foreign periodicals in the arts and allied fields, including *Film Culture, Film Quarterly, Films in Review, Sight and Sound.* Arrangement is alphabetical by author and subject. Through 1977, articles on film listed under "Moving Pictures" and its subdivisions. Film reviews listed under "Moving Picture Reviews—Single Works." Beginning 1978, consult "Motion Pictures." Book reviews indexed by author and subject. Quarterly, with two-year cumulations.

IC11. *British Humanities Index.* London: 1962–.
Indexes around 300 scholarly British journals by topic. Includes *Sight and Sound* and general magazines that review and discuss film. Supersedes *Subject Index to Periodicals,* 1915–61.

IC12. *Facts on File: World News Digest with Index.* New York: 1940–. Weekly.
This information service digests the week's news. Two entries in index: "Motion Pictures—Obituaries" and "Motion Pictures—Top Grossing Films," make this useful for film research. With date of event one can then go to the *New York Times* or any major newspaper for full story. This index runs about two weeks behind, whereas the *Times Index* runs many weeks behind. Through 1974, *Facts on File* also listed "Motion Pictures—New York Releases," a very useful feature, but this entry was dropped in 1975.

IC13. *Humanities Index.* New York: H. W. Wilson, June 1974–.
Resembles *Readers' Guide* (see no. IC18) in format, but indexes more scholarly journals, including *Cinema Quarterly, Film Comment, Film Journal, Film Library Quarterly, Film Quarterly, Sight and Sound.* Subjects and authors listed in one alphabet; consult the heading "Moving Pictures." Quarterly, with annual cumulations. Continues *Social Sciences and Humanities Index* (1965–May 1974) and *International Index to Periodicals* (1907–65).

IC14. *Index to Little Magazines.* Chicago: Swallow Press, 1900–67.
Index to selected list of literary periodicals. Authors and subjects in one alphabet. Consult heading "Moving Pictures" or individual names. Number of titles indexed varies from volume to volume, reflecting instability of "little" magazine. Annual.

IC15. *International Bibliographie der Zeitschriftenliteratur.* Osnabruck: 1965–.
Commonly abbreviated *IBZ.* Subject index to more than 7,600 periodicals in German and other major languages. Entries in German, with cross-references from English and French forms. For general articles on moving pictures check heading "Film (*Kunstwerk*)"; otherwise, check individual names. No book reviews. Author index.
Merges two earlier indexes: *Bibliographie der deutschen Zeitschriftenliteratur* (1896–1964), which indexed about 4,500 important German periodicals of all kinds; and *Bibliographie der*

fremdsprachigen Zeitschriftenliteratur (1911–64), which indexed 1,400 periodicals in non-German languages. Both are similar to *IBZ*.

New York Times Index. See no. H7.

IC16. *Newspaper Index: Los Angeles Times.* Wooster, Ohio: Bell and Howell, 1972–.

The *Los Angeles Times* gives superior coverage to the movie industry and its people, particularly in obituaries. Index organized by subjects and personal names. Under subjects, consult headings "Motion Pictures and Motion Picture Industry" and "Motion Pictures—Reviews." Entries arranged chronologically. Personal names section, arranged alphabetically, includes news items as well as obituaries. Computer produced, based on microfilm edition of newspaper. Issued monthly, then cumulated annually; runs about six weeks behind.

Newspaper Index also indexes, separately: *Chicago Tribune, New Orleans Times-Picayune,* and *Washington Post.* Prior to 1972, the *New York Times Index, New York Times Obituaries Index* (see no. G9), or *Facts on File* (see no. IC12) should be consulted.

IC17. Public Affairs Information Service. *Bulletin.* New York: 1914–. Weekly.

Usually cited as *PAIS*. Indexes books, periodical articles, documents, pamphlets, reports of public and private agencies, and the like. Excellent for economic and administrative aspects of film industry. Consult heading "Moving Pictures." Weekly, with quarterly and annual cumulations.

IC18. *Readers' Guide to Periodical Literature.* New York: H. W. Wilson, 1900–.

Indexes American periodicals of general and popular nature, by subject and author. Each entry gives author, title, periodical name, and date of issue. General articles on film indexed under "Motion Pictures" and its subdivisions. For film criticism see "Motion Picture Reviews—Single Works"; films arranged alphabetically by title. Before May 1977, consult "Moving Pictures." Articles about individuals listed by subject's name.

See the *Popular Periodical Index* (Camden, N.J.: Rutgers University, 1973–) for articles and reviews in such magazines as *Crawdaddy, New York Magazine, Playboy, Rolling Stone.* Check entries under "Motion Pictures."

ID. Periodical Locations

The lists given here will help track down a particular periodical. Most libraries will copy articles upon request—for a fee and with some delay. But this service can solve many problems. The prime source for locating periodicals in American and Canadian libraries is the *Union List of Serials* with its supplement, *New Serial Titles* (nos. ID1 and ID2). Bowles has gathered this information for some film periodicals in his *Index* (no. H2).

Bowles, S. E. *Index to Critical Film Reviews in British and American Film Periodicals.* "Union List of Periodicals," pp. 767–773. See no. H2.

New York (City). Public Library. Research Libraries. *Catalog of the Theatre and Drama Collections, Part II: Theatre Collection: Books on the Theatre.* Lists film journals under "Cinema—Periodicals." See no. DC4 and DC5.

ID1. *Union List of Serials in Libraries of the United States and Canada.* 3d ed. New York: H. W. Wilson, 1965.

Abbreviated *ULS*. Comprehensive list of serials published throughout the world; gives locations in U.S. and Canadian libraries. Serials listed alphabetically, by title or issuing body (e.g., society, university, institution, municipality, etc.), along with brief publishing information. Lists titles up to 1950; continued by:

ID2. *New Serial Titles: Supplement to the Union List of Serials.* Washington, D.C.: Library of Congress, 1961–.

Same format as *ULS*, above. Picks up serials that have begun publication since 1950.

ID3. *British Union Catalogue of Periodicals: A Record of the Periodicals of the World.* . . . 4 vols. and Supplement. London: Butterworths Scientific Publications, 1956.

Lists periodicals held by British libraries, dating from 17th century to 1955, by title or issuing organizations. Resembles *ULS* (above) except that it uses keyword filing. Handy for verifying titles that cannot otherwise be located in *ULS*.

International Federation of Film Archives. *Catalogue collectif des livres et périodiques publiés avant 1914.* See no. DC2.

J. Dissertations

Dissertations provide detailed research on specific topics. Their greatest value for most film students will be their bibliographies. The scholar who compiled such a bibliography most likely surveyed every useful source relating to the subject. The film student need only update this list.

Few libraries buy many dissertations. Any title that is described in *Dissertation Abstracts* (no. J1) or is listed in its index (no. J2) can be ordered directly from University Microfilms, Ann Arbor, Mich. Most libraries that have *Dissertation Abstracts* will have order forms; otherwise consult the "How to Obtain Dissertation Copies" page in front of any volume.

J1. *Dissertation Abstracts International.* Ann Arbor, Mich.: University Microfilms, July 1969–. Monthly.

Abstracts dissertations submitted to University Microfilms by institutions participating in its cooperative microfilming program. Arranged by discipline, then university. Subject and author index in each issue; indexes cumulate annually, but are late. Since vol. 27, divided into two sections: (1) Humanities and Social Sciences, and (2) Sciences and Engineering. Work on film is classified under such categories as "Speech-Theater" or "Psychology." Continues *Dissertation Abstracts* (vols. 12–29, 1952–June 1969) and *Microfilm Abstracts* (vols. 1–11, 1939–51). Indexed by:

J2. *Comprehensive Dissertation Index, 1861–1972.* 37 vols. Ann Arbor, Mich.: Xerox University Microfilms, 1973–.

Cumulative index for *Dissertation Abstracts International* (above) and its predecessors, covering 1861 through 1972. Keyword subject indexes; that is, principal words in each title are arranged alphabetically within broad subjects. Work on film in vols. 18–19: Psychology; vols. 29–30: Language and Literature; vol. 31:

Communications and the Arts. Vols. 33–37: author index. Supplemented annually.

J3. Fielding, Raymond. "Theses and Dissertations on the Subject of Film at U.S. Universities, 1916–: A Bibliography." *Journal of University Film Association,* 1968, 1969, 1972, 1974. First listing of theses and dissertations on film (vol. 20, no. 2, 1968) spans 1916 through 1967: covers eight universities, includes 386 titles, Second bibliography (vol. 21, no. 4, 1969) covers 32 institutions, adds 107 titles. Third bibliography (vol. 24, no. 3, 1972) lists 162 titles. Fourth bibliography (vol. 26, no. 3, 1974) lists 352 titles from 65 universities. A cumulated bibliography is in preparation that will index by subject.

Gottesman, R., and Geduld, H. M. *Guidebook to Film.* See no. A3.

Reinert, C. *Kleines Filmlexikon.* See no. B19.

Subject Index

Letter-plus-number following subject entry refers to item number in bibliography.

ACADEMY AWARDS, B14, CA17, CA20, CB7, CB9, EC2, EC3, ED12, FC24, H7 *(See also* AWARDS)
Academy of Motion Picture Arts and Sciences: A9, EE10
AFRICAN FILM, CA15, EA5, FA6, FB1, FC8
AFRO-AMERICAN FILM, *(See* BLACKS IN MOVING PICTURES)
AMERICAN FILM, EA9, EB11, EB12, EB13, EB14, EB15, EB16, EB17, FA6, FB33, FB34, FB35, FB36, FB37, FB38
American Film Institute, CA18
ANIMATED FILM/CARTOONS, EA2, ED8, FC6, FC7, FC8, FC11, H9
ARCHIVES/RESEARCH CENTERS, A3, A10, CA4, CA13, CA16, CA18, CB1, CB2, CB3, CB4, CB6, CB10, EE10
Asquith, Anthony, EC12
L'Avant scène du cinéma, EE9
AWARDS, A3, B14, CA2, CA4, CA8, CA10, CA17, CB9, EC2, EC3, ED12, G8, G19, H7

BIOGRAPHIES, B2, B6–B8, B11, B13, B14, B17, B19, B23, CA9, CA14, CA20, DA9, DB3, FB2, FB10, FB11, FB13, FB15, FB21, FB23, FB26, FB30, Section G, IC3, IC4, IC6, IC7
BLACKS IN MOVING PICTURES, DA8, EC11, FC1, FC2
BOOKSTORES, A3, A11, CA13, DC6
BRITISH FILM, A4, CA5, CA14, CA15, EA8, EA10, EB3, EG1, FA6, FB7, FB8, FB9, FB10, FC14, IA7, IA9
British Film Institute, DC1, EA2, EA8

Cahiers du cinéma, EE9

CANADIAN FILM, CA8, CA15, CB1, CB6, CB13, EB2, EB16, EB17, H8, IA11
Canadian Film Institute, A9
Capra, Frank, EC12
Carné, Marcel, EC12
Center for Advanced Film Studies, CA18
Chaplin, Charles, EC11
CHINESE FILM, EA5, FA6, FB2
Cinema, EE9
Cinema Quarterly, IC13
Clair, René, EC12
Crawdaddy, IC18
CREDITS, by picture title, B14, B23, CA1, CA2, CA3, CA8, CA10, CA11, CA14, CA19, CA20, CA21, DA15, Section EA, Section EB, EC1, EC5, EC10, EC13, ED3, ED8, ED12, G17, H3, H4, H5, H7, IA2, IA12
CREDITS, for art direction/designers, B6–B8, CA10, EA3, EC1, EG5, FB23, G4–G5, G13, G17
CREDITS, for cinematographers, B6–B8, CA3, CA9, CA10, EA3, EC1, EC6, EG5, FB23, FC27, G4–G5, G11, G13, G17, H7
CREDITS, for composers/music directors, B6–B8, CA3, CA9, CA10, CB9, EA3, EC1, EC7, EG5, FC13, FC14, FC15, FC17, FC18, FC27, G4–G5, G13, G17, H7
CREDITS, for directors, B3, B6–B8, B14, CA3, CA7, CA8, CA9, CA10, CA13, CB1, CB9, EA9, EA10, EC1, EC8, EC9, EC10, EC11–EC12, EC15, ED2, ED5, ED6, ED7, ED8, FA3, FA17, FA19, FB11, FB14, FB23, FC27, G2, G4–G5, G6, G8,

G11, G13, G17, G18, H3, H7
CREDITS, for editors, CA9, CA10, EC1, EC3, EG5, G13, G17, H7
CREDITS, for independent Film Makers, CB1, CB9, ED6, ED7, FC25, FC26, FC34, H7
CREDITS, for performers, B2, B3, B6–B8, B14, CA3, CA8, CA9, CA10, CB9, EA3, EC1, EC5, EC13, EC14, EC15, FB23, FC27, G4–G5, G8, G10, G11, G12, G17, G18, G19, G20, H7
CREDITS, for producers, B14, CA3, CA9, CA10, CB1, CB9, EC1, EC15, EF1, G2, G4–G5, G6, G8, G13, G17, G18, H7
CREDITS, for screenwriters, B6–B8, CA3, CA9, CA10, CB9, EC1, EC2, EC4, FB23, FC27, G2, G4–G5, G6, G8, G11, G13, G17, H7
CREDITS, for special effects, FC24, G17, H7
CREDITS, for supporting players, CB9, G1, G8, G10, G19, G20, H7
CREDITS, for women filmmakers, CB9, ED5, ED7, FC34, G14, H7
CRITICISM (Cited), section D, FC30, H6, H10, section IA, section IC (esp. IC3, IC4, IC6, IC7)
CZECHOSLOVAKIAN FILM, FB3, FB4, FB6

DISSERTATIONS, A3, B19, DC4, DE3, DE5; Section J
DISTRIBUTORS, A3, A6, A8, A11, CA2, CA4, CA5, CA10, CA16, CA19, CB8, EA5, EB18, Section ED, FC34
DOCUMENTARY FILMS, CA8, EA2, EA5, EA7, EA8, EB8, EB15–EB17, EC3, EC8, ED2, ED3, ED4, ED5, ED7, ED8, FB32, FC3, FC5, FC13, FD12, G11, H3, H9
Dovzchenko, Alexander, EC11
Dreyer, Carl, EC12

EAST EUROPEAN FILM, EA5, FB3, FB4, FB6, G11

EDUCATIONAL FILM, CA4, EB16–EB17, EB18, ED7, ED9, IC8
Eisenstein, Sergei, FD5
EUROPEAN (WEST) FILM, A10, B6–B8, EA9, EA10, EA11, Section EB, EC9, EE10, FA1, FA6, FA18, FA20, Section FB, FC2, FC8, FC31, FC32, G6, G13
EXPERIMENTAL/UNDERGROUND FILM, ED2, ED6, ED8, ED11, FB37, FC25, FC26, IA5, IC9

FESTIVALS, A3, B10, CA1, CA2, CA4, CA6, CA8, CA13, CA14, CA16, CB14, IA2, IA3
Film Comment, IC13
Film Culture, IC10
Film Daily, CA9, CA10
Film Journal, IC13
Film Library Quarterly, IC13
Film Quarterly, IC10, IC13
FILM SCHOOLS AND COURSES, A3, CA12, CA13, CB10
FILM SCRIPTS (Cited), A1, A2, A7, CB13, DA3, DA5, DA9–DA10, DA12, DB1, DC1, DC3, DC4–DC5, Section EE, FA10, FD6, FD18, H2, IA1, IA2
Films in Review, IC10
FINNISH FILM, FB29
Flaherty, Robert J., EC11
Ford, John, EC11
FRENCH FILM, CA1, CA2, DA6, DE3, EA9, EA10, EB4, FA6, FB11, FB12, FB13, FB14

GERMAN FILM, DE4, DE5, EB5, FB15, FB16, FB17, FB18, G11
Griffith, D. W., EA10, EB13, EC11

Hitchcock, Alfred, EC11
HUNGARIAN FILM, FB3, FB4, FB5, FB6

ILLUSTRATIONS, B6, B10, B12, B13, B16, CA11, CA20, CB7, EG1, EG2, FA13, FB34, FD14

ILLUSTRATIONS, Indexed, B3, B14, EB8
INDIAN FILM, EA5, FA6, FB19, FC8
INTERNATIONAL FILM, B10, B13, B16, CA6, CA13, CA14, CA15, CB2, CB4, CB5, CB10, CB12, DA13, DA14, DB3, EA3, EA4, EF10, Section FA, FC3, FC5, FC6, FC8, FC13, FC29, G2, G4–G5, G12, G17
ITALIAN FILM, B6–B8, CA3, CA19, DA6, EA9, EB6, EB7, EB8, EB9, FB20, FB21, FB22, FB23, FC28

JAPANESE FILM, EA5, FA6, FB24, FB25, FB26, FC28

Lang, Fritz, EC11
LITERARY SOURCE, A4, CA3, CA10, CA14, CA19, DA15, EA3, EB3, EB8, EB11, EB15, EB16, EC1, EC2, EE6, Section EF, G17
Los Angeles Times, H4, IC16
Lubitsch, Ernst, EC11

Méliès, Georges, EC11
Murnau, F. W., EC11
Museum of Modern Art, A9, DA15, EE10
MUSIC IN MOVIES, A5, CB8, EC7, FC12, FC13, FC14, FC15, FC16, IC5
MUSICALS, EB12, EB16, EF9, FC8, FC11, FC17, FC18, H8
MYSTERY/CRIME/SPY FILMS, FC19, FC20, FC21

New York Magazine, IC18
New York Public Library, DA15, DC4–DC5
New York Times, CB9, H1, H4, H7, H8, IC12
NEWSREELS, EA7, EA8, EB15, ED2, FC4

OBITUARIES, CA20, G3, G8, G9, IC12, IC16
Ophuls, Max, EC12

PERIODICAL LISTS, A1, A2, A3, A5, A6, A7, A8, CA4, CA8, CA13, CA14, CB1, DA1, DA2, DA11, DC3, DC4–DC5, FC30, FD6, FD9, H2, H9, Section IB, IC1, IC3, IC4, IC6, IC7
Playboy, IC18
PLOT SUMMARIES, CA2, CA8, CA11, EA8, EA10, EA11, EB2, EB3, EB4, EB11, EB13, EB16–EB17, Section ED, Section EG, H5
PORTRAIT GALLERY, CA1, CA2, CB9, EB13, G1, H7
PRIMARY SOURCE MATERIAL, CB3, CB4, CB6, CB10, CB13, DC1, DC2, DC3, DC4, FA8, FD11
Pudovkin, Vsevelod I., EC11, FD10

RATINGS, EA1, EG4, IA7, IA9
REMAKES, EF8, EF10
REVIEWS, CA10, CB9, DA15, Section H, Section IA, Section IC
Richter, Hans, EC11
Rolling Stone, IC18

SCANDINAVIAN FILM, EA9, EA10, FB28
SCIENCE FICTION, FC8, FC9, FC10
SERIALS, EA9, EB15, EC8, ED8, EF8, FC22, FC23, FC31
SHORT FILMS, CA1, CA8, EA1, EA5, EA7, EB4, ED2, ED3, ED4, ED5, ED9, FC13, H3
Sight and Sound, IC10, IC13
SILENT FILMS, EA1, EA8, EA10, EA11, EB3, EB12, EB13, EB14, EB15, EC8, Section FA, FB33, FB34, FB36, FB37, FD1
SONGS FROM MOVIES, EG4, FC11, FC12, FC13, FC17, FC18
SOVIET UNION FILM, EB10, FB3, FB6, FB30, FB31, FB32
SPANISH/LATIN AMERICAN FILM, B10, DA6, EA5
SPECIAL EFFECTS, FC24, FC26, H9
STATISTICS, B14, CA8, CA10, CA14, CA20, CB12, IA12, IC12

Sternberg, Josef von, EC11
STILLS (SOURCES), A3, CB8, CB10, CB11, DC3, DC4, EE11, H9
STOCKSHOT MATERIAL, CA4, CA16, CB2
Stroheim, Erich von, EC11
STUDIOS/PRODUCERS, A3, B23, CA9, CA10, CA14, CA15, CA16, CB9, EA9, EB13, EB14, EB15, EB16–EB17, EC1, EC15, FB23, H7
SWEDISH FILM, FB27, FB28
SWISS FILM, B19, CA2

TECHNICAL ASPECTS, B4, B12, B21, Section FD12–FD19, IA10
TELEVISION FILMS, CA8, CA21, EA1, ED3, ED12, EE4, EG4
TERMS/GLOSSARIES, A3, A4, A5, A6, A7, B1, B2, B3, B4, B5, B11, B13, B15, B17, B18, B19, B20, B21, B22,
B23, FD6, FD8, FD12, FD15, FD16, FD17, FD18
THEATER & FILM, FD9, FD10, FD11
TITLE CHANGES (alternate/translated/variant titles), A4, B13, EA1, EA2, EA4, EA11, EB9, EB11, EB15, EC2, EC5, EC9, EF1–EF2, EF6, EF8, FA12, FB26, FC8, FC27, G17, H8, IC3, IC6

U.S. Library of Congress, A9, CA18, DA15, DE8–DE9, EB14, EB15, EB16–EB17, FA13

Vigo, Jean, EC12
Village Voice, H4, IC1

WESTERNS, FC11, FC27, FC28, FC29, FC30, FC31
WOMEN IN FILM, ED5, ED7, FC32, FC33, FC34

Author/Title Index

Letter-plus-number following author or title refers to item number in bibliography.

A

Aaronson, Charles S., CA14
Academy Awards, CB7
Academy Awards Oscar Annual, CA17
Academy of Motion Picture Arts and Sciences, EC1, EC2, G1
Academy of Motion Picture Arts and Sciences. *Bulletin*, EC1
Academy Players Directory, G1
Aceto, Vincent J., IC3
Actor Guide to the Talkies, EC5
Alphabetical Guide to Motion Picture, Television..., B12

Alternative Press Index, IC9
Alternatives in Print, ED11
Amberg, George, H1
American Cinema: Directors and Directions, EC10
American Cinematographer, B4
American Cinematographer Manual, B4
American Film Criticism, from the Beginnings..., H10
American Film Directors, H10
American Film-Index, EB13
American Film Institute, CA12, EB11

American Film Institute Catalog of Motion Pictures Produced . . . U.S., EB11
American Folklore Films and Videotapes, ED4
American Movies Reference Book, B14
American Newsreel, FC4
American Society of Cinematographers, B4
American Theatrical Arts, CB13
Anderson, Joseph L., FB24
Annotated Bibliography of New Publications in the Performing Arts, DB1
Annuaire du cinéma et télévision, CA1
Annuaire du spèctacle: cinéma..., CA2
Annuario del cinema italiano, CA3
Approach to Film Study, A1
Armes, Roy, FB11
Arnell, Richard, FC16
Arnheim, Rudolph, FD1
Aros, Andrew A., EF2
Art Index, IC10
Art of the Film, FD8
Artel, Linda J., ED2
Ash, Rene L., EC3
Audiovisual Market Place, CA4
Audiovisual Script Writing, FD18
Avant-scène du cinéma, IA1
Awake in the Dark, H10

B

Babitsky, Paul, FB30
Baddeley, W. Hugh, FD12
Baer, D. Richard, EA1
Balazs, Bela, FD2
Bardeche, Maurice, FA1
Barnet, Sylvan, B1
Barnouw, Erik, FB19, FC3
Barrett, Gillian, IB1
Barry, Iris, FA1
Basic Books in the Mass Media, DA1
Bassotto, Camillo, DA13, EE10
Batty, Linda, IC1
Bauer, Alfred, EB5
Bawden, Liz-Anne, B16
Bean, Robin, IA7
Beattie, Eleanor, CB1

Beginning of the Biograph, FB36
Behind the Screen, FA8
Belknap, S. Yancey, IC5
Bellour, Raymond, G2
Berman, Morton, B1
Bessy, Maurice, B2
Best Film Plays of 1943–1944, EE3
Best Film Plays of 1945, EE3
Best Moving Pictures Of 1922/23, EE3
Best Pictures, 1939/40, EE3
Bianco e nero, IA2
Bibliografia generale del cinema, DA14
Bibliografia nazionale italiana, DE7
Bibliographic Index, DB2
Bibliographie de la France, DE3
Bibliographie générale du cinéma, DA14
Bibliographie internationale cinéma, DB3
Bibliographie international du cinéma et de la télévision, DA6
Bibliography of Film Librarianship, DA4
Bibliothéques et musées des arts du spectacle dans le monde, CB4
Biographical Dictionary of Film, G18
Biographical Dictionary of the Cinema, G18
Biographical Encyclopedia & Who's Who of the American Theater, G8
Biography Index, G3
Bioscope, EA2
Birkos, Alexander S., FB31
Björkman, Stig, FB27
Blacks in American Films, FC1
Blacks in American Movies, DA8
Blacks in Black and White, FC2
Blue Book of Hollywood Musicals, FC11
Bluestone, George, FD3
Blum, Eleanor, DA1
Bobker, Lee R., FD4
Bogle, Donald, FC1
Bohn, Thomas W., FA2
Bone, Edith, FD2
Book Library Bibliography, DB4
Book Review Digest, DD1
Book Review Index, DD2
Books about Film, DA7

Boussinot, Roger, B3
Bowles, Stephen E., A1, H2
Bowser, Eileen, CA18, EB12, FB34
Brasillach, Robert, FA1
British Cinema, FB8
British Film and Television Year Book, CA5
British Film Catalog, EB3
British Film Institute, DB4, DC1, EA2, EA8, EC11, EC12, ED3, FB29, H3, IA9, IB1
British Film Music, FC14
British Film Yearbook, CA5
British Humanities Index, IC11
British Museum. *General Catalogue of Printed Books*, DE1
British National Bibliography, DE2
British National Film Catalogue, ED3
British Union Catalogue of Periodicals, ID3
Brochier, Jean-Jacques, G2
Brodbeck, Emil E., FD13
Brosnan, John, FC24
Broughton, George, DA11
Brownlow, Kevin, FB33
Brownstone, David M., H4
Bucher, Felix, FB15
Bukalski, Peter J., A2
Bulletin of Screen Achievement Records, EC1
Burto, William, B1
Burton, Jack, FC11, FC12
Butler, Ivan, EG1

C

Cahiers du cinéma, IA3
Calendar of International Motion Picture and Television Events, CA6
Calendar of Motion Picture and Television Events . . . U.S., CA6
Callenbach, Ernest, IA6
Canadian Feature Films, EB2
Canadian Film Institute, CA8, EB2
Catalog of the Theatre and Drama Collections, DC4–DC5

Cataloging and Classification of Cinema Literature, A9
Catalogo Bolaffi del cinema italiano, EB6–EB7
Catalogue collectif des livres et périodiques, DC2
Catalogue des périodiques français et étrangers consacres au cinéma, IB4
Catalogue of Soviet Feature Films, EB10
Catalogue of the Book Library of the British Film Institute, DC1
Cawkwell, Tim, G17
Center for Southern Folklore, ED4
Centro Sperimentale di Cinematografia, G4, IA2
Character People, G20
Chardans, Jean-Louis, B2
Charensol, Georges, EA3
Chicorel, Marietta, EE1
Chicorel Theater Index to Plays in Anthologies. . . , EE1
Chittock, John, CB2
Christeson, Frances, DA2
Chronologie du cinéma mondial. . . , EA6
Cine Books, DC6
Cinéma, EA3
Cinema and the Negro, EC11
Cinema Beyond the Danube, FB8
Cinema Booklist, DA9
Cinema Booklist Supplements, DA10
Cinéma français (Jeanne & Ford), FB12
Cinéma français (Sadoul), FB14
Cinema: Historical, Technical, and Bibliographical, A12
Cinema in Britain, EG1
Cinema in Finland, FB29
Cinéma italien, FB21
Cinema, the Magic Vehicle, EG3
Cinemabilia, DC6
Cinemages, IB2
Cinémas africains en 1972, FB1
Cinémathèque de Belgique, IB3
Cinématographie française, EB4
Clarke, Charles G., B4
Clason, W. E., B5

Author/Title Index / 137

Closely Watched Films, FB4
Cohen, Joan, DA3
Cohen, Louis H., FB30
Collecting and Enjoying Old Movies, CB8
Collecting Classic Films, CB8
Collins, Maynard, CA8
Combs, Richard, H3
Comprehensive Dissertation Index, J2
Concise History of the Cinema, FA3
Continued Next Week, FC22
Corliss, Richard, EC4, IA4
Costner, Tom, CA16
Council on International Nontheatrical Events, CA6
Cowie, Peter, CA13, EA4, FA3, FB27, FB29
Crist, Judith, EG4
Critical Index, IC4
Crowther, Bosley, EG2
Cumulated Dramatic Index, IC2
Cumulative Book Index, DE10
Current Film Periodicals in English, IB5
Cyr, Helen W., EA5

D

Daisne, Johan, EF10
Daniel Blum's Screen World, CA20
David, Nina, CA21
Dawson, Bonnie, ED5
Day, Peter, FC16
de la Roche, Catherine, EC12
Denby, David, H10
Deutsche Bibliographie, DE4
Deutsche Nationalbibliographie, DE5
Deutscher Spielfilm Almanach, EB5
Dianying, FB2
Dickinson, Thorold, FD15
Dictionary of Film Makers, G13
Dictionary of Films, EA11
Dictionary of Literary, Dramatic and Cinematic Terms, B1
Dictionary of 1,000 Best Films, EG5
Dictionary of the Cinema, B11
Dictionnaire des cinéastes, G13

Dictionnaire des cinéastes contemporains, G6
Dictionnaire des films, EA11
Dictionnaire des oeuvres de tous les temps..., EF4
Dictionnaire des personnages littéraires et dramatiques, EF5
Dictionnaire du cinéma, G2
Dictionnaire du cinéma et de la télévision, B2
Dictionnaire du l'audio-visuel, B18
Dictionnaire filmographique de la littérature mondiale, EF10
Dimmitt, Richard B., EC5, EF1
Directors Guild of America, CA7
Directory of Members, CA7
Dissertation Abstracts International, J1
Dizionario del cinema italiano, FB23
Dizionario letterario Bompiani delle opere..., EF3
Documentary, FC3
Documentary Film, FC5
Drama Bookshop, DC6
Drama Scholars' Index to Plays and Filmscripts, EE9
Dramatic Index, IC2
Druxman, Michael B., EF8
Durgnat, Raymond, FB7
Dwoskin, Stephen, FC26

E

Eastern Europe, FB3
Edera, Bruno, FC6
Edison Motion Picture Myth, FB36
Educational Film Guide, EB18
Educational Film Library Assoc., EB18, ED8
Eisenschitz, Bernard, FA20
Eisenstein, Sergei, FD5
Eisner, Lotte H., FB16
Elements of Film, FD4
Elsevier's Dictionary of Cinema, Sound and Music, B5
Emergence of Film Art, FA5

Emmens, Carol A., CB3
Enciclopedia dello spettacolo, B6–B9
Enciclopedia ilustrada del cine, B10
Encyclopedia of Mystery and Detection, FC21
Encyclopédie du cinéma, B3
Encyclopédie du cinéma par l'image, B3
English-Russian Dictionary of Photography and Cinematography, B20
Enser, A.G.S., EF6
Esnault, Philippe, EA6
Essay and General Literature Index, DB5
Everson, William K., FC28
Expanded Cinema, FC26
Eyles, Allen, FC27

F

Fabulous Fantasy Films, FC10
Facts on File, IC12
Fawcett, Marion, IA8
Feature Films, 1921–1930, EB11
Feature Films, 1961–1970, EB11
Feature Films on 8mm and 16mm, ED8
Fédération Internationale des Archives du Film (FIAF), DB3, DC2, IC6
Feldman, Harry, EC12
Feldman, Joseph, EC12
Fenin, George N., FC28
FIAF Index, IC6
FIAF Periodical Indexing Service, IC6
Fidell, Estelle A., EE7
Fielding, Raymond, FC4, FC24, J3
Film, FA9
Film Acting, FD10
Film. . . . An Anthology. . . , H10
Film and its Technique, FD17
Film & TV Festival Directory, CB14
Film and Television Study Center, DC3
Film and the Public, FA10
Film and Theatre, FD9
Film as Art (Arnheim), FD1
Film as Art (Writer's Program), DA15
Film Buff's Bible of Motion Pictures, EA1
Film Canadiana, CA8

Film Comment, EC4, EC6, IA4
Film Composers in America, EC7
Film Criticism, H6
Film Culture, IA5
Film Daily, CA9, CA10
Film Daily Directors Annual and Production Guide, CA9
Film Daily Production Guide and Directors Annual, CA9
Film Daily Year Book of Motion Pictures, CA10
Film Directors: A Guide to Their American Films, EC8
Film Directors Guide: Western Europe, EC9
Film e la sua storia, DA13
Film Evaluation Guide, EB18
Film Form, FD5
Film in Sweden, FB27
Film Index: A Bibliography, DA15, IC7
Film Is . . . The International Free Cinema, FC26
Film Literature Index, IC3
Film-Makers' Cooperative Catalogue, ED6
Film Music, FC15
Film Notes, EB12
Film Programmers' Book List, ED1
Film Programmer's Guide to 16mm Rentals, ED2
Film Quarterly, A10, IA6
Film Research, A2
Film Resource Centers in New York, CB3
Film Review, CA11
Film Review Digest, H4
Film Review Digest Annual, H4
Film Review Index, IC8
Film Scripts, EE2
Film Scriptwriting, FD18
Film Sense, FD5
Film Students Index to the National Board of Review Magazine, IA8
Film Study: A Resource Guide, A6
Film Technique, FD10
Film TV Daily Yearbook of Motion Pictures and Television, CA10
Film: The Creative Process, FD7

Author/Title Index / 139

Film Till Now, FA18
Film Title Index, EA2
Film User's Handbook, A8
Film Viewer's Handbook, A11
Film Vocabulary, B22
Film Year Book, CA10
Filmarama, EC13
Filmdex, IC3
Filmed Books and Plays, EF6
Filmfacts, H5
Filmgoer's Companion, A4
Filmkünstler A-Z, G11
Filmlexicon degli autori e delle opere, G4-G5
Filmlexicon, piccola enciclopedia cinematografica, B17
Filmographic Dictionary of World Literature, EF10
Filmographie universelle, EA9
Filmography of the Third World, EA5
Films and Filming, IA7
Films by and/or about Women, ED7
Films in Review, IA8
Films—Too Good for Words, ED9
Filmschauspieler A-Z, G12
Finnish Cinema, FB29
First Twenty Years, FA13
Five C's of Cinematography, FD14
Flaming Years, EC13
Florence. Biblioteca Nazionale Centrale. *Catalogo cumulativo...*, DE6
Focal Encyclopedia of Film and Television Techniques, B21
Ford, Charles, FA6, FB12, G6
Foremost Films of 1938, EE3
Formidable Years, EC13
Forthcoming Books, DB6
Forty Years of Screen Credits, EC14
Fox, Stuart, EA7
Fraenkel, Heinrich, FB18
France: An Illustrated Guide..., FB13
Franck, Irene M., H4
French Cinema since 1946, FB11
French Film, FB14
From Caligari to Hitler, FB17
From Reverence to Rape, FC32

Full Length Animated Feature Films, FC6

G

Garbicz, Adam, EG3
Garrett, George P., DA11, EE2
Gassner, John, EE3
Geduld, Harry M., A3
Gelfman, Jane R., EE2
General Bibliography of Motion Pictures, DA14
Gerlach, John C., IC4
Gerlach, Lana, IC4
German Cinema, FB18
Germany, FB15
Gertner, Richard, CA14
Gessner, Robert, FD6
Gifford, Denis, EB3, FB8
Goodgold, Ed, FC23
Gotham Book Mart and Gallery, DC6
Gottesman, Ronald, A3
Graham, Peter, B11, FA4
Graves, Jane, IC3
Great British Picture Show, FB10
Great Films: Fifty Golden Years of Motion Pictures, EG2
Great Gangster Pictures, FC19
Great Science Fiction Pictures, FC9
Great Spy Pictures, FC20
Great Western Pictures, FC31
Griffith, Richard, EC12, FA18, FB34, FB35, FC5
Group for Film Study, IB2
Guide to College Courses in Film and Television, CA12
Guide to College Film Courses, CA12
Guide to Critical Reviews, H8
Guide to the Literature of the Motion Picture, DA2
Guide to the Performing Arts, IC5
Guidebook to Film, A3

H

Halas, John, FC7
Halliwell, Leslie, A4
Hampton, Benjamin B., FB35
Hampton Books, DC6

Handbook of Basic Motion-Picture Techniques, FD13
Handbook of Canadian Film, CB1
Handling, Piers, CA8
Hanisch, Michael, G12
Hardison, O. B., EE2
Hardy, Forsyth, FB28
Harrington, Curtis, EC11
Haskell, Molly, FC32
Haunted Screen, FB16
Heinzkill, Richard, H6
Hembus, Joe, FC29
Hendricks, Gordon, FB36
Hennebelle, Guy, FB1
Henstell, Bruce, H10
Hibbin, Nina, FB3
Hillier, Jim, FB29
Hippenmeyer, Jean-Roland, FC13
Histoire du cinéma, FA1
Histoire du cinéma, art et industrie, FA12
Histoire du cinéma français, FB14
Histoire du cinéma mondial des origines à nos jours, FA19
Histoire encyclopédique du cinéma, FA6, FB12
Histoire générale du cinéma, FA20
History of Motion Pictures, FA1
History of the American Avant-Garde Cinema, FC25
History of the American Film Industry, FB35
History of the British Film, FB9
History of the Cinema, FA16
History of the Film, FA1
History of the Movies, FB35
History of World Cinema, FA17
Hochman, Stanley, H10
Hollywood Musical, FC17
Hollywood Quarterly, IA6
Hollywood Screenwriters, EC4
Houston, Penelope, IA9
How to Locate Reviews of Plays and Films, H9
How to Organize and Run a Film Society, A11
How to Read a Film, A7

Huff, Theodore, EC11
Humanities Index, IC13
Humphrys, Barbara, ED1
Huntley, John, FC14, FC16

I

IFTC Directory of International Film and Television Organizations, CB5
Index de la cinématographie française, EB4
Index of American Popular Music, FC12
Index to Characters in the Performing Arts, EF9
Index to Critical Film Reviews..., H2
Index to Full-Length Plays, EE4
Index to Little Magazines, IC14
Index to 16mm Educational Films, EB18
Indian Film, FB19
Institut des Hautes Études Cinématographiques, EA9, IB4
International Bibliographie der Zeitschriftenliteratur, IC15
International Encyclopedia of Film, B13
International Federation of Film Archives (FIAF), DB3, DC2, IC6
International Federation of Library Associations, CB4
International Film and Television Council, CB2, CB5
International Film and Television Yearbook, CA5
International Film Guide, CA13
International Index to Film Periodicals, IC6
International Index to Multi-Media Information, IC8
International Index to Periodicals, IC13
International Liaison Center of Film and Television Schools, CB10
International Motion Picture Almanac, CA14
International Television Almanac, CA14
Internationale Filmbibliographie, DA5
Introduction to the American Underground Film, FC26
Ireland, Norma O., EE4
Italian Cinema (Jarratt), FB20

Italian Cinema (Leprohon), FB21
Italian Cinema Today, FB22

J

Jackson, Arthur, FC17
Jacobs, Lewis, B13, FA5, FB37
Japan, FB26
Japanese Cinema, FB25
Japanese Film, FB24
Japanese Movies, FB25
Jarratt, Vernon, FB20
Jarvie, I. C., Da11
Jazz in the Movies, FC13
Jazz sur Films, FC13
Jeanne, René, FA6, FB12
Jewell, Richard B., EE11
Jewish Films in the U.S., EA7
Jobes, Gertrude, FB38
Jones, Karen, IC6
Journal of the Society of Motion Picture Engineers, IA10

K

Kauffmann, Stanley, H10
Kemp's Film and Television Directory, CA15
Kemp's Film and Television Year Book, CA15
Kindlers Literatur Lexikon, EF7
Kinetoscope, FB36
Kino, FB32
Kleines Filmlexikon, B19
Klinowski, Jacek, EG3
Knight, Arthur, CB9, FA7
Koszarski, Richard, EC6
Kowalski, Rosemary R., FC33
Kracauer, Siegfried, FB17
Krishnaswamy, S., FB19
Kula, Sam, DA4

L

Lahue, Kalton C., CB8, FC22
Lamparski, Richard, G7
Larry Edmunds Bookshop, DC6
Laurence, Frank M., EE5
Lauritzen, Einar, EB13

Lawson, John H., FD7, FD18
Lebensold, Peter, IA11
Lee, Walt, FC8
Leonard, Harold, DA15
Leprohon, Pierre, FB21
Lester, Sandra, IA8
Levitan, Eli L., B12
Leyda, Jay, EC11, FB2, FB32, FD5
Leyland, Eric, A12
Liehm, Antonin J., FB4
Liehm, Mira, FB4
Light and Shadows, FA2
Limbacher, James L., A5, ED8, EF8, FC15
Limelight Bookstore, DC6
Lindgren, Ernest, FD8
Liveliest Art, FA7
Lizzani, Carlo, EB8
Los Angeles Times, IC16
Low, Rachael, FB9
Lundquist, Gunnar, EB13

M

Ma L'Amore No, EB9
McAnany, Emile G., A11
Macaulay, Richard, EE3
McCallum, Heather, CB6
MacCann, Richard D., CA18, IC3
McCarty, Clifford, EC7, EE6
McClure, Arthur F., G20
McGill, Raymond D., G8
MacGowan, Kenneth, FA8
Make It Again, Sam, EF8
Malkin, Audree, DC3
Maltin, Leonard, EG4
Man and the Movies, DA11
Manchel, Frank, A6
Manvell, Roger, B13, FA9, FA10, FB9, FB18, FC7, FC16
Manz, H. P., DA5
Mapp, Edward, FC1
Martin, Marcel, FB13
Mascelli, Joseph V., FD14
Mast, Gerald, FA11
Mayer, Arthur, FB34

Media Review Digest, IC8
Meeker, David, FC13
Mehr, Linda, DC3
Mekas, Jonas, IA5
Men with the Movie Cameras, EC6
Meyers, Warren B., G1
Michael, Paul, B14, CB7
Microfilm Abstracts, J1
Millar, Gavin, FD15
Million and One Nights, FA15
Mirror for England, FB7
Mitry, Jean, DA6, EA9, FA12
Monaco, James, A7, B15, DA7
Montagu, Ivor, FD10
Monthly Film Bulletin, H3
Morris, Peter, EA11, EB2, G13
Most Important Art, FB4
Motion Picture Almanac, CA14
Motion Picture and Television Almanac, CA14
Motion Picture Directors, G14
Motion Picture Empire, FB38
Motion Picture Film Editor, EC3
Motion Picture Market Place, CA16
Motion Picture Performers, G15
Motion Picture Performers: Supplement 1, G16
Motion Pictures: A Catalog of Books, Periodicals..., DC3
Motion Pictures, Catalog of Copyright Entries, EB15
Motion Pictures 1894-1912, EB14
Motion Pictures from the Library of Congress Paper Print Collection, EA10
Motion Pictures, Television and Radio: A Union Catalogue of Manuscript..., DC3
Moulds, Michael, IC6
Moulinier, Pierre, IB4
Movie Magic, FC24
Movies, FB34
Movies and Society, DA11
Movies on TV, EG4
Moving Image, FD6
Moving Picture World, EB13
Multi-Media Reviews Index, IC8

Munden, Kenneth W., EB11
Muro, Fred F., CB8
Museum of Modern Art, EB12

N

Nachbar, John G., FC30
National Board of Review of Motion Pictures, IA8
National Film Archive. Catalogue, EA8
National Film Library Catalogue, EA8
National Film Theatre, EC12
National Information Center for Educational Media (NICEM), EB18
National Society of Film Critics, H10
National Union Catalog, DE9
Neergaard, Ebbe, EC12
Negro in Films, FC2
Nemeskúrty, István, FB5
New Film Index, IC7
New Index Series, EC12
New Movies, IA8
New Serial Titles, ID2
New Wave: Critical Landmarks, FA4
New York (City) Public Library, DC4–DC5
New York Times Directory of the Film, CB9
New York Times Film Index, H7
New York Times Film Reviews, H7
New York Times Film Reviews, A One-Volume Selection, H1
New York Times Guide to Movies on TV, EG4
New York Times Index, G9, H7
New York Times Obituaries Index, G9
Newspaper Index, IC16
Nichols, Dudley, EE3
Nicoll, Allardyce, FD9
Niver, Kemp R., EA10, FA13
Noble, Peter, CA5, EC11, EC12, FC2
Notable Names in the American Theatre, G8
Novels into Film, FD3
Novotny, Ann, CB11

O

O'Leary, Liam, FA14

Author/Title Index / 143

One Good Film Deserves Another, EF8
Origins of the American Film, FB36
Osborne, Robert, CA17
Oxford Companion to Film, B16

P

Parade's Gone By, FB33
Parish, James R., EC8, EC9, FC9, FC19, FC20, FC31
Parker, Norton S., FD18
Parlato, Salvatore J., ED9
Parmentier, Ernest, H5
Pasinetti, Francesco, B17
Penzler, Otto, FC21
Performing Arts/Books in Print, DA12
Performing Arts Libraries and Museums of the World, CB4
Performing Arts Resources, CA18
Periodical Holdings 1974, IB1
Perry, Edward S., IC7
Perry, George, FB10
Perry, Ted, CA18
Pessis-Pasternak, Guitta, B18
Pickard, R. A. E., EG5
Picture Sources 3, CB11
Pitts, Michael R., EC8, FC9, FC19, FC20, FC31
Play Index, EE7
Popular Periodical Index, IC18
Poteet, G. Howard, EE8
Powers, Anne, DA8
Primary Cinema Resources, EE11
Primer for Filmmaking, FD16
Principles of Cinematography, FD19
Prinet, Jean, IB4
Produzione Italiana, CA19
Public Affairs Information Service: *Bulletin,* IC17
Published Radio, Television and Film Scripts, EE8
Published Screenplays, EE6
Pudovkin, V. I., FD10

Q

Quarterly of Film, Radio and Television, IA6

Queval, Jean, EC12

R

Rad Jewish Film Archives, EA7
Ragan, David, G10
Ramsaye, Terry, CA14, FA15
Ramsey, Verna, EC1
Rangoonwalla, Firoze, FB19
Readers' Guide to Periodical Literature, IC18
Redi, Riccardo, DA14
Reference Guide to Audiovisual Information, A5
Reference Guide to Fantastic Films, FC8
Reference Guide to Film Information, A5, EF8
Rehrauer, George, A8, DA9, DA10
Reichow, Joachim, G11, G12
Reilly, Adam, IB5
Reilly, Charles P., IA8
Reinert, Charles, B19, G11
Reisz, Karel, FD15
Renan, Sheldon, FC26
Répertoire mondial des filmographies nationales, EB1
Répertoire mondial des périodiques cinématographiqes, IB3
Retrospective Index to Film Periodicals, IC1
Rhode, Eric, FA16
Richie, Donald, FB24, FB25
Rigdon, Walter, G8
Rimberg, John, FB30
Rise of the American Film, FB37
Road, Sinclair, FC5
Roberts, Kenneth H., FD16
Robinson, David, FA17
Robinson, William R., DA11
Rondi, Gian L., FB22
Rondolino, Gianni, EB6, EB7, FB23
Rose, Ernest, CB10
Rotha, Paul, FA18, FC5
Roud, Richard, EC12
Rovin, Jeff, FC10

144 / Moving Pictures

S

Sadoul, Georges, EA11, EC11, FA19, FA20, FB14, G13
Sakharov, Aleksandr A., B20
Salem, James M., H8
Samore, Theodore, DA3
Samples, Gordon, EE9, H9
Sampson, Henry T., FC2
Sarris, Andrew, EC10
Savio, Francesco, EB9
Scandinavian Film, FB28
Schenker, Susan, DA7
Scheuer, Steven H., EG4
Schlosser, Anne G., DC3
Schoolcraft, Ralph N., DA12
Schuster, Mel, G14, G15, G16
Screen Achievement Records Bulletin, EC1
Screen World, CA20
Screenplay from "The Jazz Singer"..., H8
Seventy-five Years of Indian Cinema, FB19
Sharp, Harold S., EF9
Sharp, Marjorie Z., EF9
Sharples, Jr., Win, FD16
Sherwood, Robert E., EE3
Short History of the Movies, FA11
Sight and Sound, IA9
Sight and Sound, Index Series, EC11
Sightlines, ED8
Silent Cinema, FA14
Silva, Fred, IC3
Sitney, P. Adams, FC26
Smith, John M., G17
Smith, Sharon, FC34
SMPTE Journal, IA10
Social Sciences and Humanities Index, IC13
Society of Motion Picture and Television Engineers, IA10
Soggetti e sceneggiature, EE10
Songs from Hollywood Musical Comedies, FC18
Sovexportfilm, EB10
Soviet Cinema, FB31
Soviet Cinema, Film and Photography, FB30
Soviet Film Industry, FB30

Special Libraries Association, CB11
Speed, F. Maurice, CA11
Spigelgass, Leonard, EC2
Spottiswoode, Raymond, B21, FD17
Sprecher, Daniel, ED10
Stage to Screen, FD11
Standard Glossary for Film Criticism, B15
Steele, Robert S., A9
Steinbrunner, Chris, FC21
Stern, Seymour, EC11
Stewart, John, EC13
Stoil, Michael J., FB6
Storia del cinema italiano, EB8
Strenge, Walter, B4
Stromgren, Richard L., FA2
Subject Guide to Books in Print, DB6
Subject Index to Periodicals, IC11
Superfilms: An International Guide to Award Winning Educational Films, ED9
Svensson, Arne, FB26, FB27
Swain, Dwight V., FD18
Sweden, FB27

T

Take One, IA11
Taylor, John R., FC17
Taylor, T. Allan, FC19, FC20, FC31
Technique of Documentary Film Production, FD12
Technique of Film Animation, FC7
Technique of Film Editing, FD15
Technique of Film Music, FC16
Technique of Special Effects Cinematography, FC24
TV Feature Film Source Book, ED12
TV Guide to the Movies, EG4
TV Movies, EG4
TV Season, CA21
Theater Arts Library (UCLA), DC3
Theatre Collection: Books on the Theatre, DC4–DC5
Theater Library Association, CA18
Theater Resources in Canadian Collections, CB6

Theory and Technique of Playwriting and Screenwriting, FD18
Theory of the Film, FD2
Thiery, Herman, EF10
Thompson, Howard, EG4
Thomson, David, G18
Title Guide to the Talkies, EF1–EF2
To Be Continued..., FC23
Toeplitz, Jerzy, A10
Toms, Coons, Mulattoes, Mammies and Bucks, FC1
Truitt, Evelyn M., G19
Turconi, Davide, DA13, EE10
Twenty Best Film Plays, EE3
Twenty Years of Silents, EC15
Twoney, Alfred E., G20

U

Ulrich's International Periodicals Directory, IB6
Ulrich's Quarterly, IB6
UNESCO, CB4, CB12
Unesco Statistical Yearbook, CB12
Union Catalogue of Books and Periodicals..., DC2
Union List of Serials in Libraries, ID1
U.S. Copyright Office, EB14, EB15
U.S. Library of Congress. *Catalog of the Books Represented...*, DE8
U.S. Library of Congress. *Films and Other Materials for Projection*, EB17
U.S. Library of Congress. *Library of Congress Catalog*, EB16
University Film Association, CB10, J3
University Film Association. *Journal*, J3
University Film Study Center, ED1

V

Valenzuela, Louis, CA8
Van Nooten, S. I., B22
Vardac, A. N., FD11
Variety, IA12
Veinstein, André, CB4
Venturini, Franco, DA14
Versatiles, G20
Vincent, Carl, DA14
Visionary Film, FC26
Vocabulaire du cinéma, B22
Voiculescu, Ervin, EB1
Vreeland, Frank, EE3

W

Wald, Jerry, EE3
Walls, Howard L., EB14
Warfield, Nancy, IA8
Weaver, John T., EC14, EC15
Weaver, Kathleen, ED2
Weinberg, Herman G., EC11
Weiner, Janet, A11
Weiss, Ken, FC23
Western, FC27
Western Films, FC30
Western: From Silents to the Seventies, FC28
Western-Lexikon, FC29
Whatever Became of...?, G7
Wheaton, Christopher D., EE11
Wheeler, Leslie J., FD19
"Who is That?" The Late Late Viewers Guide..., G1
Who Was Who on Screen, G19
Who Wrote the Movie and What Else Did He Write?, EC2
Who's Who in Hollywood, G10
Wid's Year Book, CA10
Williams, Robert, A11
Willis, John, CA20
Winchester, Clarence, B23
Wir vom Film, G11
Woll, Allen L., FC18
Women and Film, FC33
Women Who Make Movies, FC34
Women's Films in Print, ED5
Women's History Research Center, ED7
Wootten, William P., EC11
Word and Image, FB5
Work Projects Administration, DA15
World Cinema, A Short History, FA17
World Communications, CB12
World Directory of Stockshot and Film Production Libraries, CB2

World Encyclopedia of the Film, G17
World Film and Television Study Resources, CB10
World Film Encyclopedia, B23
World Filmography, EA4
World List of Film Periodicals and Serials, IB3
Wrigley, Maurice J., A12

Writers Guild of America: West, EC2
Writer's Program: New York, DA15

Y-Z

Yearbook of Motion Pictures, CA10
Young, William C., CB13
Youngblood, Gene, FC26
Zwerdling, Shirley, CB14